Tales of an African Beekeeper

From 'The Life of King Henry the Fifth'

"Therefore doth heaven divide

The state of man in divers functions,

Setting endeavour in continual motion;

To which is fixed, as an aim or butt,

Obedience: for so work the honey-bees,

Creatures that by a rule in nature teach

The act of order to a peopled kingdom.

They have a king and officers of sorts;

Where some, like magistrates, correct at home,

Others, like merchants, venture trade abroad,

Others, like soldiers, armed in their stings,

Make boot upon the summer's velvet buds,

Which pillage they with merry march bring home

To the tent-royal of their emperor;

Who, busied in his majesty, surveys

The singing masons building roofs of gold,

The civil citizens kneading up the honey,

The poor mechanic porters crowding in

Their heavy burdens at his narrow gate,

The sad-eyed justice, with his surly hum,

Delivering o'er to executors pale

The lazy yawning drone."

William Shakespeare

Peter L Clark

TABLE OF CONTENTS

HONEY PRODUCTION

THINGS TO WATCH OUT FOR

APPENDICES

Tales of an African Beekeeper

Peter L. Clark

During spring (September to October), one area in Kirstenbosch transforms from drab greyish-green shrubs to these glistening, dazzling mounds of colour. They are the Vygies (pronounded fay-gh-ease), also known as Mesembs, Midday Flowers or Ice Plants. They are various species of *Lampranthus, Drosanthemum* and *Ruschia,* small shrubby succulents that belong in the family Mesembryanthemaceae and mostly come from the semi-arid regions of South Africa, such as the Karoo.

ISBN: **1469966719**
ISBN-13: **978-1469966717**

Version 7.3

Order Enquiries:

For South African country sales: enquiries@peterclark.co.za

http://www.peterclark.co.za

International: https://www.createspace.com/3780193

International http://www.amazon.com

Available on Kindle and Paperback

DEDICATION

Now in the sunshine years of my life and at the age of 75 years, I dedicate this book to my daughter, Susan, who always prompted me to write some story of my life, and my son-in-law, Jeremy, who boldly collated some of my material from my annual beekeeping courses together with some personal experiences to compile this book.

Secondly to my dear wife, Mary, who sat about into the early hours of many mornings, waiting for my return back to her from beekeeping excursions to unknown destinations – into bushveld areas, forests, and far away places for pollinations of farmers' crops. There were no cell phones to keep one in close contact, but I always assured her and my two young children that I would not leave the planet.

To my son, Andrew, who shares with me outings to the bees and some of the adventures that go with them. Always concerned as to my whereabouts – where I am going, what route I will be using, and at what time I should be home – a great support to me.

Foremost, and at the top of my list, I extend my dedication to my dear father who after the age of 65 years then devoted 21 years to assisting me in all aspects of the craft.

To my two laborers Piet and Jacob, I thank you fellows, because without your faithfulness I could not have proceeded.

Peter Clark, Springs, South Africa, June 2012.

Peter L Clark

PREFACE

It is intended that this book will stimulate the enquiring mind of those who are aware that there is such a creature as a bee and that there are people who devote their lives to working with bees.

There are folk who have desired to keep bees and perhaps this read will whet their appetite and encourage them to get started. There are also those who have started and are not aware of the in-depth nature of the subject that could take them far beyond their wildest dreams.

To the seasoned old beekeeper there will be that knowing grin that similar experiences also occurred in his life, but hopefully he will learn something new from these pages.

Perhaps the book will soften the hearts of those who hate and detest bees, those whose only desire is to kill them at first sight. However there are those who have lost a loved one due to a bee sting and they must be pardoned from wishing to take revenge. But the book might ease their burden and hopefully they will glean a better understanding of this marvelous creature of God's creation.

The chapters are short and to the point and are designed for a reference at a glance and for that reason the author seeks pardoning for minor instances of repetitiveness.

The chapters on incidences and episodes of bee disasters are true occurrences in which the author was involved. There were many, many more – far too many to describe within the pages of this book. They have been related merely to illustrate the ongoing life of a beekeeper.

Hopefully the book will reach the gardeners, farmers and horticulturists, and all lovers of the great outdoors who daily look upon a foraging bee and marvel at God's mighty creation.

FOREWORD

I have known Peter Clark for some twenty years, in which time I have come to know a man with great passion for his bees and all of the different facets of his trade as a beekeeper. Peter's accumulated wisdom in all matters 'bee' has been acquired the only way of true wisdom – the hard way.

As I have heard him tell tales of adventure and hard work, trips in the middle of the night to the middle of nowhere, I have wanted to capture some of them. I have also looked at the articles and training material that he has compiled and refined over many years, and prevailed upon him to collate all of this.

In the pages of this book you will find Peter sharing of this wisdom in his unique style, mixing story and information in a conversational way. There are so many stories that have not made it into the book for space reasons, and maybe that is motivation for a second book, but I first have to convince him that people would really like to hear his tales.

The book consists of a compilation of new, revised, and updated material from his published articles, his training courses and talks, the people he has met, and the encounters he has had through his work.

'Tales of an African Beekeeper' is written for gardeners, farmers, beekeepers and students. The garden enthusiast will find much to explain the behaviour of these small co-workers of theirs; the farmer will be taken a few steps further than their current knowledge of the bee and its usefulness; and the novice and experienced beekeepers will find it a valuable addition to their 'toolbox'. Students of agriculture, horticulture and entomology will find that the bee is far more fascinating than the textbooks will reveal.

The book is written in an easy to follow style, with short concise chapters which make it both an easy read and a handy reference book that is easy to dive in and out of. This is not written as a manual - there are many good theoretical and instructional beekeeping books out there - but as a reflection on many practical lessons learned in the past sixty years with the bees.

As you turn to the opening pages of the book, I hope that you will enjoy the journey through the strange and industrious world of the bee and the beekeeper.

Jeremy Farrell, Cape Town, South Africa, May 2012

"The only reason for making a buzzing-noise that I know of is because you're a bee...The only reason for being a bee that I know of is making honey....and the only reason for making honey is so I can eat it."
Winnie the Pooh in A.A. Milne's 'The House at Pooh Corner'

1   Introduction

Welcome to the world of the honey bee, *Apis mellifera adonsoni*, the bearer of sweet burdens. Researchers and archeologists record that they have been around since around 20,000 BC.

Beekeeping to the farmer is another way of life and to the hobbyist a most enjoyable and interesting craft carried on by male, female, young and old. It is a subject that extends far beyond just keeping bees, but to the flora, the trees both indigenous and exotic of our land, and to the many crops that provide food on the table. As bees are found foraging on strange flowers, the inquisitive beekeeper goes to all ends to find the names of such plants and so his general knowledge accumulates and extends far beyond all his expectations.

As a farming venture, beekeeping tops the list. Bees are a productive livestock that need no feeding, no watering, no nursing of sicknesses to health, no expensive maintenance. All they ask of their owner is space to work and store honey. They are the most dedicated, free, non-complaining labor force of any employer. Love them, enjoy them and they will motivate you to work long hours, often late into the night, to assure you of great success of your beekeeping career.

All who commence beekeeping start somewhere and as this book is about my life as a beekeeper, allow me to start at the very beginning.

At the tender age of 11, my very first encounter with bees was at the Convent of the Sacred Heart, Klerksdorp, where my 8 year old brother and I were bi-weekly boarders along with others around our ages, only going home every second week-end.

The sisters at the convent took pity on us and tried to make our school week-end stays as pleasant as possible.

One sister, a German nun, kept bees and she delighted to kit me up in an oversize outfit and show me into a beehive. As I look back on my life, I question as to whether this was God's angel to set me up in my latter years as a bee farmer.

Page on and I invite you to enjoy the book. It is merely an account that touches the very perimeter of a most enjoyable and in-depth craft of keeping bees.

"How doth the little busy bee
Improve each shining hour,
And gather honey all the day
From every opening flower."
~ *Isaac Watts*

2 The honeybee

The earliest records of man's association with bees dates back to 15000 BC with a painting in Spain of two women removing honey from a high up cave with multitudes of bees flying around them. There are records around 3000 BC of Egyptians floating primitive beehives on barges along the Nile River. A Roman author has writings of two brothers keeping bees commercially just north of Rome with annual honey yields of 2500 kg. There is a rock art painting in the Southern Drakensburg of two people climbing a rope ladder and removing honey from a cave.

So the mighty bee has been around for a long, long time. It is a fascinating flying and working insect that man has been able to harness to work for him in a very big way. Loved by many thousands of beekeepers throughout the world, it is the principal pollinator of all seed producing flowers, grasses, fruits and most of our indigenous plants and trees. Without bees all these plants would not exist.

The worker bee is a barren female. She works from first light to last light and on moonlight nights when the

Boekenhout and the Marula trees of the bushveld[1] secrete their nectar. As the sun sets and the darkness descends, the bees will be seen working in the moonlight. There are no bosses, no unions, no starting and knocking off times, no Sundays and no public holidays, no time off to see the doctor or the dentist, no annual leave, no retirement and no pension schemes. Even on rainy days there is much to do inside the hive, such as wax building and general cleaning. And so on and on they go, and all they ask of the beekeeper is space to work and store the honey.

The worker bee is usually yellow banded, but some are darker and slightly grey. She has five eyes, two compound eyes and three small eyes across the front of her head. She has a long tongue that can reach down far into the deeply located nectar cells of most flowers and she has two stomachs. One stomach is part of her digestive system and the other is for carrying nectar to the hive.

She has a pair of arms that contain combs on her forearms, a pair of pivoting centre legs and a pair of strong hind legs as her main supporting legs that contain two sticky patches to which she sticks pollen, also known as pollen baskets. She has four wings, one pair for general flying and the second to assist with the heavy loads of pollen or nectar when transporting back to the

---

[1] The South African word "veld" means the vast, open, mostly uninhabited grassland countryside, and "bushveld" means the countryside dominated by large varieties of indigenous trees. These areas abound in large varieties of wild flowers and wild animals large and small.

hive. Tucked away in a sheath at her rear end she carries her defence weapon – her sting, within quick and easy reach.

Let us accompany our little lady on a foraging flight. Should the swarm need pollen, her mission is to fetch pollen and likewise for nectar, should the swarm need honey. She does not collect nectar and pollen on the same flight. Suppose the Iceland poppies are flowering – they secrete pollen in the early morning. She will even break into a large poppy bud to be the first at the flower. She rolls around in the flower collecting pollen onto the hairy surface of her thorax. She reverse flies up and out of the poppy and being a female, she is able to perform a number of operations simultaneously.

While flying to the next flower she combs the pollen off her hairy thorax with her arms, passes it to her middle legs and then to her pollen baskets. On one flight she will collect poppy pollen only and not mix the pollen of a different plant such as a nasturtium. To and fro to the hive she flies, perhaps 20 trips in a day depending how far the hive is from the pollen source.

The house bees will have selected a special place in the hive as a pantry to store the pollen and not just in any cells scattered in the hive, so that when they are seeking pollen to consume, they know exactly where to go, and so too with the nectar that is foraged. Into the pantry cell area she speedily goes, reverses into a cell and scrapes the pollen off the baskets with the claws on her hind legs. The house bees pack the pollen in an orderly fashion and after the cell is filled, they seal it with a thin layer of honey to preserve it until needed.

Collecting nectar, the bee extends her tongue deeply into the nectar cells of the flower, draws the nectar into her carrying stomach, flies to the hive and regurgitates it to a house bee. The house bee in turn passes it to another, and then to another, until the liquid thickens to the thickness of honey. As in the gathering of pollen, she does not gather nectar from two different types of flowers.

Heat and draughts created by the bees, especially at night, drive off the excess moisture of the honey, and when the percentage of moisture is reduced to 9% they cap the cell with a thin layer of wax.

During the process of making honey, the bees will collect seven litres of nectar to produce one litre of honey – just imagine 140 litres of nectar to produce approximately 55 x 500 gram bottles of honey, such as one finds on the supermarket shelves.

So, have love and respect for our little ladies of the honey industry. Before one kills a bee, marvel at the wonders of this little creature, preserve it, protect it and give it just a second chance. When a bee mistakenly loses direction and accidently flies into a room, the cry goes out, "Kill it!", where it should rather be, "Save it, a daughter of the land!"

"Concerning the generation of animals akin to them, as hornets and wasps, the facts in all cases are similar to a certain extent, but are devoid of the extraordinary features which characterize bees; this we should expect, for they have nothing divine about them as the bees have."

~ Aristotle 384 BC – 322 BC

3   The Queen's life cycle

We the beekeepers of Africa and South Africa, can be proud that our queens are the best strain of bees in the world. They are strong and disease resistant.

There are two strains of bees in South Africa namely, Apis mellifera scutellata that occurs north of Port Elizabeth, and Apis mellifera capensis which occurs in the Cape.

The only function of the scutellata queen is to increase the size of the swarm, and to replace the continual loss of workers. Should she fail to perform, the swarm will die out. However the workers of Apis mellifera capensis are able to lay eggs to produce workers and from one of these eggs a capensis queen could develop and in this way the bees are able to replace a lost or failing queen of Apis mellifera capensis, but this is not the case with the scutellata strain of bees.

Therefore the bottom line reads, good performing queens produce good performing workers and good honey yields are obtained, whereas poor performing queens produce poor honey yields.

With this background in mind, let's consider the life cycle of a scutellata queen.

She emerged from a wax constructed cell about 22mm long from an egg laid by her mother. The nurse bees had transferred this egg into the queen cell and fed it a special high protein mixture of royal jelly and pollen. After eight days the cell is packed with royal jelly and capped, and after a further five days she emerges as a beautiful light lemon colored queen. She takes her nuptial flight and is fertilized on the wing. She starts her egg laying function at 23 days old and performs this sole function daily for about three years.

As the queen goes about her daily work, she is surrounded by nurse bees that continually preen her and a contingent of house cleaner bees that go before her to polish and clean the empty used cells for her to lay her eggs. A good performing queen is able to lay up to two thousand eggs in a twenty-four hour day, or her own weight in eggs.

This entourage continually follows her around over the surface of the brood frames in the breeding areas that are being utilised. These bees continually pick up a pheromone which she secrets from her abdomen and they pass on this pheromone to other bees in the swarm. This odour is distinct to each individual swarm. Should a foreign bee, not of this pheromone, attempt to enter the hive the guard bees will attack it.

So this is Africa, no space for passengers in the swarm. These attending nurse bees notice that Mother Queen does not smell too good anymore and her egg laying performance is failing. They convey to the rest of the swarm that things are no longer so good up front, and something has to be done about the situation. Mother Queen, now nearing three years old, which is her ultimate life span, is like any elderly person who thinks she is still up to scratch, but the young generation knows otherwise and they start taking action.

The wax builders start building about ten queen cells to develop new queens. A single egg is transferred by the nurse bees to each cell and a concentrated layer of royal jelly is placed around each egg.

Mother quickly becomes aware of this change of attitude to her, and so she sends out scout bees to find a new abode. She knows well that the new queen will be stronger than her and she will be assassinated by her rival. The scouts have been faithful to her and will not let her down, so out they go. They search around perhaps up to five kilometers away to be sure that they are not within the foraging range of her previous abode. A suitable place is found and they fly up and down in a tunnel pattern formation perhaps ten meters wide, passing and greeting one another as they fly. Some old faithful house bees now join this force and they start cleaning and preparing this new abode to accept their queen – after all she too had served them well so why let her down in her hour of greatest need.

Twelve days later, the capped cells are about to hatch, mother hears the piping calls of the new queens and she is ready to fly. She has been on diet for the past twelve days and like a spring chicken she emerges from the hive. Her followers all gorge themselves with honey before they fly. There is a swirling and whirling about the outside of the hive. Her faithful followers all gather around in the air, and led by the scouts they make a bee-line to their newly selected and prepared abode, hence the expression "to make a bee-line" – to move in a direct direction as quickly as possible.

This move over five kilometers is very rapid and within about 20 minutes they are in their new abode. Carrying the excess honey that the workers had gorged before they departed enables them to immediately set about building new combs in order to store new nectar and pollen, and within a week the queen is in condition to start laying eggs again. However because of her failing, the swarm will not develop to any great strength and unless a new queen is raised, the swarm will die out.

However, the other scenario that could happen is that as soon as the nurse and attendant bees notice that the mother queen is failing and the pheromone is not up to scratch, they "ball the queen". They form a tight ball around the queen. This action increases the temperature within the ball and the queen dies of overheating and suffocation. The nurse bees then proceed to raise a new queen as described above.

An obvious question to ask is why the nurse bees did not ball her in the first place when they noticed that she was failing? It could be that she was still strong enough to start a new nest and only after she further deteriorated would they then ball her. In this way a new swarm will have been developed, which in nature's language means that the species continues to survive.

Tales of an African Beekeeper

A Tale of Uninvited guests

Our story opens on a scene on a winter's day towards the end of June in the bushveld, on a farm in the Aloe Daveyana belt that stretches across the country north of Pretoria and south of Warmbaths. Aloe Daveyana is a low growing aloe that occurs all over the bushveld and on heavily grazed bushveld farms. The flower spikes grow to about 1m tall with four or five branchlets comprising a dense beautiful profusion of pink to red flowers in clusters on the spikes that last for about eight weeks from the beginning of July to the end of August each year. During this period the beekeepers flock to these areas with as many as 3000 hives and look upon this period as the "wake-up" time for their hives for the new honey season. This is the backdrop for our story...

On a certain farm in this area, a brand new windmill had been erected. Because of the lack of wind for a longish period the windmill did not operate and a swarm of bees moved into the gearbox at the top of the windmill. It was a perfect abode for a swarm, well chosen by the scout bees at the time, high up and safe from any invasion of mankind. It was the third and final year in the life expectancy of the Mother Queen and, as in the previous two years, she remembered the sequence of events that would occur again this year. Her staff were unaware of this situation and the events to come as none of them had survived from the previous season.

And it was on this late June day that some scouting workers excitedly flew into the nest with the good news that they had noticed some aloe spikes just starting to appear at the bases of the plants. News spread rapidly through the nest and the cleaner bees and the workers, working at night in the brood area, started to move honey out of the brood area to prepare for the new laying season. Nurse bees informed Mother Queen and started to feed her royal jelly to condition her for the forthcoming breeding season. She had had her 10 weeks of rest and was eager to get into the new season.

Mother Queen then summoned all the swarm occupants to a conference meeting in the nest. They were all there – workers, guard bees, nurse bees, young newly hatched workers and the few drones that had survived the winter. The bees usually drive the old drones out of the hives in the winter to die in order that new young drones develop for the new season.

She stood on her throne, crown on her head and sceptre in her right hand to address the crowd:

"Listen to me carefully and pay attention. Within the next few days this area will be invaded by at least 150 hives of thousands of bees. I call them squatters as they will be here for the duration of the flowering of the aloes. They will fill their hives with pollen and nectar. We will have to start earlier than them and work harder and longer if we are to gather enough to see us through into the next honey flow that starts in October on the acacias, the marulas and the boekenhout. When the flowers are over they will be gone and we will be left with a mere existence. They will invade the animal drinking troughs where we normally get our water and there is to be no fighting at the drinking troughs."

She then turned to the guard bees. "I want extra security at all exposed entrances, especially at the end of the nectar flow, and extra guards on duty well into the dark and on moonlight nights. There is to be a 24 hour patrol as they, like us, fly and work in the moonlight. Under no circumstances must they gain entrance and find our honey stores as they will clean us out – we will not survive," she boomed. The meeting adjourned and the occupants were tense as they could not imagine the invasion to come.

Peace reigned for another day and night and then it happened. The following morning, just as mother had said, there were nearly 200 hives scattered all over the area and thousands of very thirsty bees already at the drinking trough even before sunrise. As there were yet flowers to open, some marauders were already looking around the windmill but the guard bees expected them and bravely defended their entrances.

A week later the flowers' spikes began to open. There were bees everywhere, two or three at each flower head forcing their way into the florets. This massive invasion lasted for a full eight weeks.

Then there appeared from nowhere, four huge two-legged creatures all dressed in white with framed and netted head gear as though from outer space. They just helped themselves to most of the honey. The workers of the squatter hives sat about their hive entrances destitute and broken-hearted – all that work and effort in vain. But their hearts and souls are strong and they will soon forget, as they have a mere five day memory, and soon, when they arrive at the citrus they will work as hard again as ever before.

The last of the flowers were open and one morning in the early spring of an August day all was quiet … the squatters had gone as quickly as they had arrived and peace and quiet prevailed again. The work effort and new honey of the windmill swarm was safe and untouched. All the bees cheered and there was great jubilation at the never ending wisdom of their noble Mother Queen.

"The careful insect 'midst his works I view,
Now from the flowers exhaust the fragrant dew,
With golden treasures load his little thighs,
And steer his distant journey through the skies."
~ John Gay

4   The beekeeper

The little honeybee is the mainstay of a 20 billion Rand industry in South Africa, covering the following main aspects:

- Production of honey

- Production of wax

- Production of propolis and other hive products for the medicinal industry

- Pollination of flowers for seed production

- Pollination of commercial honey producing crops

- Paid pollination, of non-honey producing crops.

- Production of mead

- Removal of swarms

- Development of swarms for the pollination industry.

- Control of diseases among bees

- Involvement in various training schemes to development beekeepers.

The value of bees in the pollination of crops is immeasurable. The deciduous fruit growing industry, the production of sunflower seed oil, the lucerne, onion, beans and buckwheat seed cultivation industry, all depend on bees and the list goes on and on to include our entire indigenous flora for the fruits and berries consumed by birds animals and insects. This leads to say that a person who gives up his life to serve the land as a beekeeper plays a most important and leading role in the maintenance and development of the ecology country-wide.

Beekeepers fall into the following main categories:

- Hobbyists with up to 20 hives,

- Beekeeping with over 20 and up to 100 hives would be looked upon as a good paying hobby.

- A beekeeper with over 100 and up to 250 hives would be regarded as a small commercial operator. He will need the assistance of an occasional assistant, otherwise he mainly works alone. He could sustain a fair living.

- A beekeeper with over 250 and up to 500 hives would have to operate full time employing at least one assistant in the field. He will have to employ an additional person to deal with the bottling, selling and distributing of honey if honey is his main product. He will need to add a 3 ton truck to his kit.

- Beekeepers with over 500 hives fall into the professional category and have their own association. They usually deal in bulk honey sales and get involved in pollination contracts.

Let's look at the survival of various beekeepers at different levels of each ones organization.

The hobbyist (1 to 50 hives)

He works alone with the occasional assistance of a fellow beekeeper or family member or friend. He pays no wages except a small gift or monetary hand out occasionally. He is not all that interested in costs as long as he has ample pocket money and keeps going until the money runs out.

He does not practice swarm replacement and usually has a heap of empty boxes in his back yard. He supplies honey at a cut price usually to friends and a small regular customer base. He does not migrate and local gum sites are his hunting grounds. That is how he survives.

The semi-hobbyist (51 to 200 hives, non-migratory)

At this level beekeeping is suitable for a retired pensioner where another income from investments is essential. He will need to employ at least one laborer and will always need to keep running costs as low as possible. He will need about 10 secure sites that he will have to visit at least once a month. He will need to keep proper records of "what to do next visit". His duties cover all aspects of the organization from hive maintenance, swarm replacement, cropping, extracting, bottling, selling and delivering his honey to his customers. His organization has to run on smooth well-oiled wheels as he has no time for mistakes and mishaps.

He would probably reap 4 tons of honey sold for R180,,000. His costs would be about R90,000 with an excess for his pocket of R90,000 which, for easy consideration is 50% on gross turnover. His capital investment should not exceed R300,000 to enable him to have a 30% return on capital investment. However, consider that R90,000 for his own pocket will give him a monthly income of R7,500 – rather a poor survival, but survival nevertheless.

The semi-professional (201 to 700 hives, migratory)

Assuming that there are 700 hives always in the field, he will need two assistants for the field work and a 'sales assistant' that deals with all the sales. Apart from his daily chores he will probably work 100 nights a year into the early hours of the mornings. He will need 14 holding sites each with 60 hives, from which he can make up his migratory load of 50 hives for each move migratory load.

He will need to practice a swarm replacement of 20%, about 120 hives per annum. He can expect 20 tons of honey yield, the bulk of which he will sell as bulk honey to a bottler. His gross turnover will be around R400,000 per annum, his costs will be around R250,000 and his net excess income about R150.000. This constitutes a 37% on gross turnover.

His capital investment should not exceed R1,100,000 to give him a 14% investment on capital. His monthly income will be about R12,500 – not much for all that work, but he survives.

Other considerations

Beekeeping is capital intensive and requires a very costly outlay to build up a good operating outfit. However, it is an undertaking where one can start small and grow at one's own pace of development.

Mostly the work is outdoors, often into night-time hours, so one has to be healthy and fit and not be troubled by back ailments as are so many South Africans. Hard work is the order of the day if one is to succeed.

The ability to plan ahead is essential. Goals must be set and adhered to as one needs to know what will be happening in January, twelve months hence, and then every month as the year progresses. One learns to observe what plants are flowering through the year and how one is going to get the honey from those flowers in those days. To meet these requirements the bees have to be kept up to strength at all times.

Beekeeping is successful and most enjoyable when one, with some knowledge of bees, can work with self-confidence and determination – which can only be obtained by working with another beekeeper. It is this "hands on" learning that cannot be attained from books or classroom lectures. As one meets successful and established beekeepers, one finds that most of them were taught by an established beekeeper at the outset of their careers. Therefore, no matter where a beekeeper operates, he will fall into the area of a beekeepers' association which, for his own benefit, he should join. At meetings a variety of topics are discussed, videos are shown and guest speakers are hosted. Field days are organized and a social atmosphere prevails among beekeepers sharing their experiences one with another.

NOTES

"We ought to do good to others as simply as a horse runs, or a bee makes honey, or a vine bears grapes season after season without thinking of the grapes it has borne."

Marcus Aurelius

5 Training Day

I have been running training courses for many, many years now, ranging from one day overviews, to eight month courses consisting of one Saturday per month sessions for the more advanced students. It is always interesting to see who signs up, particularly for the advanced course, and what they want to achieve. I have had young and old, corporate and retired, self-employed and unemployed. There have been students who just want to learn more about the bee, novices, would-be small business starters, and hobbyists.

In one of my recent courses I had students such as:

- Margaret[2] the Post-Graduate student doing her Masters in Entomology, who just wanted some real field experience as part of her research.

- Nadia* and her two children – Muslims who had come along to learn beekeeping so that they could produce raw honey for cultural and family events, based on their belief in the healing capabilities of pure honey. In their community there was suspicion about the purity of commercially produced honey.

---

[2] Real names not used.

- Koos* and his son Piet,* who had come along to learn a skill for Piet. I have had several such family pairs where, based on an understanding that the formal sector does not hold great employment prospects for school-leavers, they want their son to learn a 'trade'. There is always also an interest in becoming a beekeeper's apprentice, but there is a general reluctance to take on this kind of responsibility amongst the Associations' members.

- Marinda* and John* came along as they are tired of paying exorbitant store prices for the honey that they love, and want to keep a few hives in their garden in order to take off some honey every week (some municipalities allow this, but many do not).

In the past I have also had students who wanted to, and have, started making products derived from honey and wax. Although one can make a reasonable living as a professional beekeeper, there is a higher profit per kilo to be made as you start to produce related products in smaller formats.

Other beekeepers are running training for government and municipalities. Some of these have to be accredited trainers before government will contract them, and since the cost of attaining accreditation is higher than I would recoup in a reasonable time, I have not gone the government route.

Certain government departments are training 'beekeepers' because they interpret the bee business as follows:

Hives = Honey = Money

Actually the formula is a little more complicated, at a minimum it is more like the following:

(Hives + Equipment + Kit + Truck + Workshop + Premises + Experience + Forage + Bees + Knowledge + Market + Processing + Employees + Effort) = Yield.

Whether that 'Yield' translates into Sales, and whether those Sales are Profitable or Sustainable, is another set of variables in itself. Unfortunately government cannot just train, and then expect people to become self-sustaining beekeepers. Some seed capital needs to be put into each project, if any sustainable success is be expected.

Some municipalities have to train up staff and emergency services personnel in order to provide bee removal services in certain areas. There are some townships and settlements which are no-go areas for many of us beekeepers. Stories of crime are enough of a deterrent when removal fees are seldom worth the effort anyway, and the costs do not offset the risks. (This is not to say that all townships and settlements are dangerous, but us old codgers are not going to take unnecessary risks.)

Water meters and electrical boards are rendered inaccessible to the meter readers by new swarms living in them, and this has to be dealt with. So, enter the municipal employee who knows how to remove bees, but nothing more. What does he do with the bees?

Anecdotal evidence makes us think that there is a growing bee problem in these areas, and the council needs to come up with a better plan, in conjunction with our Associations.

A little more on the business of bees

Earlier in this chapter I mentioned reasons that people came on my courses, and business is quite common. Whereas some of us are more traditional or mainstream honey producers, you get enterprising people all along the supply chain.

Business opportunities being taken advantage of are:

- Pure honey

- Raw honey

- Comb honey

- Honey sweets

- Cosmetics

- Wax-based products (lip balm, lubricant, polishes)

- Gift and Hospitality products

- Propolis

- Royal Jelly

There is a growing interest in the health benefits and medicinal use of honey. In New Zealand Manuka Honey is considered to have several documented medicinal properties for a range of health problems. A jar of this honey will sell for up to eight times the price of a jar of 'normal' honey.

Tales of an African Beekeeper

There is ongoing research into the general longevity of beekeepers. What is it that keeps us active and healthy for so long? Is it the honey we eat? The propolis we inhale? The pollen in the honey we work with, or the little snatch here and there of royal jelly? I am certainly not the only seventy-five year old beekeeper still working his own hives!

So, don't be shy to think about how the trusty bee can provide you with more than just a honey product and a long and healthy life. Be creative, and who knows where this great business can take you.

<u>Notes</u>

"Don't wear perfume in the garden, unless you want to be pollinated by bees."

Anne Raver

6   It's all about the kit

Failing kit puts the new beekeeper out of business the first time he opens his hive and the bees bypass his kit and sting him – usually rather badly.

One cannot stress this point enough for the benefit of the new beekeeper. So, spend the money on good quality beekeepers' equipment, obtained from a shop that sells beekeepers' equipment.

Let us start from the top and work our way downwards.

The Beekeeper's veil and headdress

There are four types of this equipment:

A separate stiff brimmed hat and an unattached veil. This is not good because there are two separate units and the fitting of the top of the veil to the hat crown can hook on the branch of a tree, slightly pull away from the crown of the hat and allow the bees into the hat area.

The second unit of veil equipment comes as a fixed hat to the veil which forms one article and is the preferred type of headdress.

Both types of veil have a short skirt attached to the bottom of the veil which ties in the front with a long string arrangement through two rings and around the bodice.

When purchasing the veil, try it on in the shop. The front depths of the veils that are sold vary in depth from the bottom of the hat to the start of the skirt which is the viewing area. Sometimes the bottom of the veil's viewing area rests on the shoulders or is bumped onto the beekeeper's shoulders which dislodges the hat and causes the veil and hat to spring upwards. When this happens the front viewing area touches the beekeeper's nose and as quick as a flash the beekeeper will be stung on the nose. Be warned and watch for this fault. If no other suitable veil is available then the beekeeper has to modify the veil in some way to suit his body.

Thirdly, there is an outfit known as a joggy. This comprises a fixed veil to hat that in turn is fitted to a light jacket. There is a zip arrangement that occurs across the front of the join of the veil skirt to the jacket portion, which allows one to release the veil and pass it over one's head when the veil is out of use. The jacket has long sleeves with elasticized cuffs that one draws over the gauntlets of the gloves. One puts on the clothing, arms first and then over one's head. On goes the hat/veil combination and finally an enclosed drawstring at the waist ties to seal off the joggy to the overalls. This article should also be baggy when fitted. The outfit is much cooler as one need only to wear a thick shirt under the joggy.

Somehow into the hat or separately one needs to wear a sweatband around the forehead especially when one wears spectacles.

Fourthly, there is a complete outfit where the veil arrangement, as in the case of the joggy, is fitted onto the overalls as one complete unit. This is by far the ultimate luxury in bee veils available. The veil skirt zips away from the overall to allow one to wash the overalls. The disadvantage of this outfit is that when one needs to replace the overall due to wear and tear, it is a major operation to remove the zip and stitch it to another new overall.

The overalls

These are to be white overalls two sizes larger than that which one would normally wear. There are two weights of material in which these overalls are made. The heavier and thicker material is preferred and there must be a collar attached and not just a rounding of the neck fitting. The overall must have a long, good quality zip. Some overalls have open pockets to the inside which enables one to removes articles from any inside pockets of other clothing. These pockets must be sown up to avoid bees entering into the overalls via the pockets.

The gloves

PVC gloves must be obtained fitted with a gauntlet that comes well up the arm. There is elastic in the top end of the gauntlet to keep the gauntlet secured well up the arm. There must be a type of material lining which has been vulcanized into the manufacture of the glove. Straight PVC or just rubber without any lining is most unsuitable. Put the gloves on in the shop and take particular notice of the stress of the glove material between the thumb and the first finger. If this is taunt and overstressed the gloves will last no time at all and must be avoided. Often times one will find suitable gloves in a hardware shop and one will have to fit the gauntlet. When utilizing a joggy, one does not need to have elasticized gauntlets fitted to the gloves.

Ladies who have small hands may have difficulty finding gloves, therefore a knitted inner glove can be worn inside the rubberized gloves. These form inner linings and absorb sweat and are comfortable to wear.

The footwear

Comfortable boots with anklets such as the army type is best. Gumboots are not good unless one has an elasticized gauntlet between the top of the boot and onto the overall below the knee. They are very hot to wear, become uncomfortable and add to the overheating of one's body.

How to dress

Start with a pair of well-fitting jeans. These jeans must be that secure that they do not work down with bending and come down inside the overall, as it is difficult to pull jeans up when they are inside the overall. Don't be ashamed to wear braces onto these jeans.

It is a good idea to wear a vest to absorb perspiration, and then a shirt and top (depending on the weather).

Next, put the overall over this lot of clobber – hence the need for an overall two sizes larger than normal. Now, on go long socks that come securely over the bottoms of the legs of the overalls and then on go the boots.

Undress the top of the bodice of the overall, arms out to fit the veil. Turn up the collar of the shirt and the undergarment and place the back short skirt of the veil over these collars and fix the veil by ending up with the tie in the front at one's belly. Put on the top section of the overalls so that the back collar of the overall covers the veil that would be resting onto one's neck and shoulders at one's neck. This is to avoid bees entering into the veil unit when one lifts one's arms to reach overhead for anything. Pull up the zip as high as it will comfortably go. Some zip clips that are supposed to keep the zip closed tend to come down, therefore one may need to safety pin the zip to prevent it from working down. The tie bows of the strings of the veil are in behind the zipped overall and cannot hook loose when working.

This is the only way to dress for beginners. It is very hot, one perspires profusely but unfortunately this is the way to start. As one becomes more confident, some beekeepers wear overalls only, a light veil, a loose veld hat and no gloves and endure a sting or two during a half hour session in the apiary.

Always keep overall and gloves clean and free from any lodged bee stings that will have dried, as the odour of the stings remain and induces the bees to start stinging before one even opens the first hive.

A Tale of 'misfit' Kit

Students on a bee course come in all shapes and sizes, the short and the tall, young and middle-aged, old, male and female, fathers and sons, mothers and daughters. They come with enquiring minds, excited and most willing to learn about the hidden secrets of the beehive but, unfortunately, they sometimes **listen but do not hear, and hear but do not listen!**

Not for the first time, I once had a student who didn't follow the earnest instructions he had been given regarding correct kit ...

It was the third 'day' of a twelve week part-time course and the time had arrived for our final kit 'dress rehearsal'. All the students lined up on the parade field dressed in new veils, overalls, shiny boots and gloves, and, armed with their bright yellow hive tools they looked good.

Above all the excited chatter, I raised my voice to call them to attention:

"Listen to me carefully. Today each one of you will open a beehive, remove and inspect two brood frames and gently replace them and close down again. The apiary is at a vacant smallholding just down the road. Next door is a nursery, and behind the plot is very inquisitive fellow and his two ridgeback dogs, and in front is a tarred road where people often walk."

"Follow me and drive to the plot and park under the trees along the northern boundary. The grass is rather thick but there are no holes or objects that could trouble you. Leave your cars open and your keys in the ignition. Should the bees harass you your escape route is to get into your car and close the windows. The claustrophobic atmosphere will force the bees to the windows and continually open and close the windows and in this way you will clear the bees away from you. You will not be able to return to the hives and will have to call it a day and I will see you next course day next month."

After we arrived and parked I immediately noticed that two students had parked at the nursery and two students along the road. This was my first failing — I should have insisted that these people park as I had instructed.

Old Quizzy and his dogs were then asked to depart from the fence as we were about to open beehives. The twenty hives were all lined up over a distance of two hundred meters and with smokers ablaze I demonstrated how to smoke, gently open, inspect, and close the hive. Slowly but positively we progressed. But the operations were too slow and the bees in the last hive got the message that they were also in line to be disturbed and they organised themselves and were waiting for us. We dosed them with extra smoke but they just came at us and war was declared.

"Retreat," I shouted, and to their cars the students fled. Quizzy and his dogs set up a dust trail, but one of the students tripped and fell in the thick grass. Because his veil was not fitted properly, it dislodged as he fell and in went the army of bees. In his endeavours to fight them off he became exhausted and lost consciousness in the grass. Another student and I lifted and pretty much dumped him onto the back of my vehicle. I poured a couple of litres of water over his face and torso and then off to the hospital we careened. When we pulled into the ambulance emergency bay, we removed his veil, emptying out about a hundred angry and confused bees that had not as yet stung him and wheeled him into the ER. He was still alive, heartbeat 56 to the minute. They pumped him full of oxygen and a saline drip and proceeded to remove the bee stings around his face, mouth, neck and ears.

The patient survived about two hundred stings. The nurses had been counting as they removed them one by one with tweezers. I, in my endeavours to help him, had received about twenty stings inside my veil.

Back at the apiary, bees that followed those students to the nursery car park, stung nursery customers. Bees also followed the students who had parked on the road, and stung three passers-by. Old Quizzy and his dogs were stung too. Then there were those students who locked their cars and could not retrieve their keys in their trouser pockets within their overalls and they were stung as well.

The unfortunate, yours truly, the course instructor and head of affairs, got marching orders to vacate the site within 24 hours!

I also learned that it might be a good idea to have an indemnity clause on my course registration forms!

"Bees work for man, and yet they never bruise
Their Master's flower, but leave it having done,
As fair as ever and as fit to use;
So both the flower doth stay and honey run."
George Herbert

7 Stings

There would be a great deal more people keeping bees if bees did not sting at all, and there would be a lot more marauding of honey which probably would have led to their extinction in these days of greed. So, the fact that bees sting and in so doing, promote a great deal of fear among the masses, is of great advantage to the beekeeper.

Why do bees sting?

Bees produce a very delightful sweet tasting commodity called honey. In fact honey is the only natural sweetener available and has a great variety of uses. It is sought after by birds, animals and humans and is freely available at no cost – all they need to do is find the bees' nests and rob all the honey. If this plundering, which removed all the bees' food supplies, continued unabated, then bees would be extinct in no time. Therefore Almighty God in His creation of the honeybee equipped her with a very powerful defence mechanism – the sting, and the agility to apply this sting rapidly and effectively. Therefore stings are used by bees to protect themselves, to protect their nest and queen, to protect their honey stores and to protect their environment.

Things that aggravate bees

The sole purpose for the presence of bees is to pollinate plants for seed and fruit production and for these reasons they are living, flying work machines. They like nothing better than to get out as early as possible in the fresh air, and work until dark every day of their working lives. Should anyone cross their paths and interfere with them they will retaliate.

Now, as we are aware that they just want to get on with their job, let's dwell on some things that aggravate bees.

How would you like someone to continually walk across your work path, and you have to constantly collide with this menacing intruder? Your temper will soon be shortened. So avoid walking across the work path of a swarm of bees.

After working 12 hours a day for most of your life and some intruder decides to help themselves to your stores, which will leave you destitute and hungry, you will surely attack, even putting your life at stake. And should the intruder attempt to injure your precious queen or injure any of your fellow workers and damage your house, you will surely strike with all your might.

Then comes along some guy on a noisy machine ploughing up the ground, or cutting the grass, or kicking up a lot of dust. Surely he will annoy you? And what about that smelly compost heap that they have built right on your doorstep, especially if they have been burning that compost and it smolders day and night. And then there is that smelly chicken run, pigsty, or dirty cow yard that stinks, especially after a rainy day or two. These are items that make bees short-tempered and, should one wish to keep bees on a plot, these hazards must be avoided.

Should bees have been working on a heavy nectar flow which has suddenly been removed, as for example when a heavy hailstorm destroys a field of cosmos, or the farmer decides to cut his entire Lucerne crop in one afternoon, which leaves absolutely nothing for the bees, they become very short tempered and will tend to sting for no rhyme or reason at all.

Warning Signs

A bee issues three warning signs before stinging. Firstly, she will buzz around the intruder, secondly, she will fly at its head, thirdly, she will strike as to sting, and if the intruder has not heeded these warnings she will sting without further ado.

So what does one do when bees go on a stinging rampage? There is absolutely nothing one can do to calm them in such cases. The only action is to take cover, put pets and livestock into sheds and under cover immediately.

At this stage let us stress that folk living on smallholdings should have some sort of bee veil and gloves. If these articles are not available, cover one's head with a blanket or large coat to simulate a moving tent when attempting to do any rescue work, bite the bullet and go out into the battle to save an animal or a person. Bees tend to target one beast or human which they can recognize they are getting the better of and will persist at that object to actually kill it. Look around for such a case and cover that object with a blanket. The next action is to calm that object and cool it down as quickly as possible with cold water. Retreat to cover as quickly as possible.

If a human being is badly stung go immediately to a hospital for help. If a pet dog is badly stung, make for the vet, and if poultry is stung to death, put them into the roasting pot for Sunday's dinner.

Bee Venom

There are three main varieties of strains of bees in South Africa, namely our normal Apis mellifera scutellata found around the Highveld and Free State, Apis capensis found in a wide belt along the Cape coast up to about East London, and Apis Litirea found along the Mozambique coastal belt. There is a small black bee of the Waterberg and Zoutpansburg mountains which is a sub species of Apis Scutellata. All these bees sting prolifically. The degree of burning sensation one gets from the various types of bees is not due to the different species but due to the different pollens of the areas where these bees forage.

Bee venom is deadly poisonous and the fractions of a milligram of bee venom discharged in a single bee sting can cause great discomfort and even death to the strongest – if he or she is highly allergic to bee stings.

Thank goodness bee sting venom comes in such small packages because should it come in the volume of a snake-bite discharge, the culprit would be dead in 10 seconds, and that goes for any old hardened beekeeper as well.

Removing Stings

Now let's consider the occasion where one gets one or two stings when walking past the swarm. Immediately scratch out the sting in a sideways action with one's finger-nail. Do not attempt to clasp the sting or touch the poison sack that will be seen attached to the sting as this only squeezes the poison quicker into the wound. The poison is drawn into the body by the capillary attraction of the blood moving around under the skin and the warmth of the body. The full poison sac empties within 20 seconds, so removing the sting should ideally be done within two seconds.

If out in the lands, it is most important to cover the sting area to conceal the odour given off by the sting, else the other bees in the area will attack to sting. Wash the sting area with cold water and cool off the wound as soon as possible. Do not touch or prod the stung area. The body tissue has become very tender and any prodding forces the venom further into a larger area around the stung area.

Normally the stung area has a burning sensation for about 15 minutes, and swelling occurs which is the body's isolation of the spread of the poison. This swelling can last for a day or two. Swelling is not classified as being allergic but itchiness, blotches, heart palpitations, throat and breathing reactions are classed as being allergic to bee sting.

Action to assist someone who has been stung

When someone has been stung, observe the person carefully. Be calm oneself, talk quietly to the patient to obtain the patient's confidence in you, and avoid creating a panic scenario. Speak slowly and with good positive conversation and reassure the patient that you will act responsibly, and all will be well. Wash the sting area with cold water and cover the sting area with a cloth or the patient's other hand. The odour of the poison will attract the next sting within a flash.

If the victim becomes flushed, cool him down by applying a cool wet cloth or jersey over the victim's head. If the victim become itchy and breaks out in pink or red blotches around his neck and throat, get him to a doctor as quickly as possible. Shakiness, shortness of breath, asphyxiation, and heart palpitations can also occur. Then move as fast as possibly to the nearest hospital, forget about the doctor.

How to minimize stinging

There comes a time when one has to work on the hives, either taking off honey or doing routine inspections. These should be joyous and exciting times for the beekeeper and should not be feared.

To begin, the beekeeper needs good bee-proof kit, (avoid any leather equipment), a good smoker with cool, clear, clean smoke. Be very gentle and work with slow positive movements, use plenty of smoke at first, and avoid killing one single bee. Work in the late afternoon, starting about half an hour before sunset and as the dark sets in. Refrain from using a light, unless there are some particular items in the hive you wish to see. Do not attempt to work when lightning is about. This upsets the bees tremendously.

For the beekeeper to avoid stinging attacks on him, he also needs to know and understand the habits of the bees and be able to read the moods that the bees are in before he starts working on them. The same colony can have different moods during the day and various colonies of the same apiary can have different moods during the same time of the day. These moods are affected by the following conditions:

If there is no honey flow on the go, the bees are idle and most workers will be at home so work on them in the late afternoon with plenty of smoke.

If there is a honey flow in progress, one can walk among the hives but not in the working flight paths, as most workers will be foraging and getting on with the job and will leave one alone. One can work on these bees during the heat of the day with minimal smoke and fight.

If the nectar flow has stopped because of a cold or rainy spell, the bees become short tempered and will be aggressive and will fly at one as one alights from one's vehicle. Work in the late afternoon using plenty of smoke.

If the nectar secretion ceases during a certain time of the day because of the particular type of plant, work (if one is able to) when the field force is working otherwise during the late afternoon and into the dark.

If there is a drought with endless dry hot days, the bees are very aggressive and if disturbed will persist in their fighting attitude into the next day or two after disturbing them so rather avoid opening any hives.

The presence of ants, a small snake, or excessive hive beetles that continually harass the bees can change the mood of a single hive in an apiary. This type of interference cannot be detected before one opens the hive and suddenly one has to deal with an angry swarm that tends to upset the rest of the apiary and the remaining hives still to be inspected.

In summary

- Always use clean white overalls. Yesterday's smelly bee-stung overalls are bad news and can set the stinging ball rolling in a very short while.

- Always use clean (non- leather) gloves.

- Work slowly with a positive action and have the planned operation in mind so as to have all the required equipment and gadgets on hand to do the job.

- In an apiary, always work from the furthest hive to the nearest hive i.e. furthest from the gate of the bee site or one's vehicle. Also avoid walking among the hives that have been disturbed and do not reopen any hives that have already been worked on.

- Do not work in stormy weather with thunder and lightning about.

- Avoid killing bees. There is nothing worse than to introduce a bee blood-stained hive tool into the next clean hive.

- Do not spill pieces of comb about the apiary.

- Always use cool smoke by burning a natural fiber product as dry gum leaves pine needles or dry bark. Add a piece of old comb or propolis into the smoker for a calming effect on the bees as well.

Ultimately the most important object of the whole exercise is to avoid being stung. Bee venom remains lodged in a beekeeper's system and eventually excessive bee-stings during a beekeeper's life will cause a bad reaction, which one day, will force him to give up beekeeping altogether.

Whilst bee sting is deemed good as a cure for arthritis, continual and repeated stings on one's hands over many years will result in deformed fingers and knobbly and painful joints in the fingers.

So, for a long beekeeping life well into your 90's avoid bee stings as much as possible.

A Tale about Willie

My fellow beekeeper friend, Willie, had a special relationship with his bees. We used to say that he lived with his bees, as if they were friends of a kind.

A famous trick of his was to sit himself down and bring his workers to him. He would do this by taking the Queen from the hive – a tricky process in itself – and cup her in his hands. By gently moving his hands around her, he would be causing her to give off pheromones that he would then 'spread' over his torso.

There he would be, sitting in his underpants as the bees slowly but surely settled on his bare skin. He would treat his face so that none settled on him there, but for the rest it was a free-for-all for his workers and he was soon totally covered. Contrary to what you would think, they would not sting him!

With his party trick over, he would be faced with how to get the bees to go home and leave him to get dressed again. Now, you try getting thousands of bees off you without causing a stir!

<u>Notes</u>

"I have somewhere seen it observed that we should make the same use of a book that the bee does of the flower; she steals sweets from it, but does not injure it"

Charles Caleb Colton

8   The smoker and its use

Smoke represents the presence of fire and when detected by the bees it is a life threat to them. Instinctively they know that fire will destroy them as wax is highly inflammable and their hive will burn very easily. They take immediate action to leave the hive and take in as much honey as each bee can carry to start a new hive after they have fled the fire.

This is the only weapon that the beekeeper has to control the bees by creating this threat of fire. Therefore he needs a good reliable smoker that will keep alive as long as there is smoker fuel burning in the fire chamber. That is to say that the smoker must not extinguish whilst there is smoker fuel in the fire chamber.

There are a number of different designs and makes of smokers on the market, ranging in three sizes, large, medium and small. The large or medium size is preferable and not the small one because the fire chamber of the small one does not hold enough fuel for even the smallest operation. The type with a heat guard around the fire chamber is the best.

The design of the smoker should have a funnel type lid and not the round dome lid with the small pipe outlet where the smoke is discharged. These smokers burn very hot, produce very hot smoke and are not robust enough with the result that the small pipe outlet breaks off rather easily. Inside the smoker and at the bottom there must be a perforated screen on small brackets to position the screen above the inlet pipe from the bellows thus preventing the fuel from choking the inlet pipe to the fire chamber.

The smoker fuel

Dry pine needles are the best fuel, delivering a cool white to light gray smoke which is the correct texture of the smoke. The disadvantage of pine needles is that they do not burn long enough and a keen eye has to be kept on the quantity of fuel in the chamber.

Corrugated cardboard cut into strips 30mm x 100mm and packed vertically is a good material but the disadvantage is that the cardboard is made with a tar substance glue which gums up the lid of the smoker resulting in a messy task to clean the inside of the lid.

Dry cow or donkey dung is good and lasts well for the work duration of any task to be undertaken. The disadvantage is that who wants to blow donkey 'drolle' over clean capped honey that is going to end up on the breakfast table.

The smoking operation

Work over your vehicle back surface or loading area.

Crimp a piece of newspaper, place it into the fire chamber of the smoker and ignite it. Do not ignite it first and then try to get it into the fire chamber of the smoker.

Then add whatever type of fuel one intends to burn. Puff the bellows and get the smoker operating properly before starting to work. Once the fire chamber heats up, the draft of the rising heat creates a chimney type of function that keeps the smoker operation ongoing. The smoker must emit white smoke which is cool smoke. Should the smoke turn to a blue color, there is a flame present in the fire chamber which makes the blue smoke a hot smoke that kills brood and bees on contact. The presence of blue smoke is an indication that the smoker needs more fuel and that the fuel is running out and the beekeeper has to pause during his operation and add more fuel to the smoker before proceeding.

With the smoker in good operation, blowing cool white smoke, first smoke around the hive and across the entrances to convey to the bees that there is a fire and then gently into both entrances. Wait approximately 30 seconds and gently puff smoke again into both entrances and into any leaky parts of the hive where bees move about. Gently prize the lid open with the hive tool and blow smoke in under the lid. Lift the lid and puff smoke over the frames.

Gently, is the password. Gently smoke, gently lift the lid, gently lift the queen excluder, and gently lift the frames, gently smoke again and again as smoke is required during the operation. Gently speak to them, no cursing or swearing at them even if they sting you. Work over the open hive with slow movements to impart to the bees – your loyal, unpaid work force – that you are there to improve their working conditions by taking their honey or attending to brood conditions in the brood chamber in order to give them more space to work, which is all that they ask for …. more space to work.

To extinguish the smoker plug the spout and lay the smoker on its side and it soon dies out. If while working with the smoker, and it is knocked over to lie on its side, it will very soon die out. Therefore always ensure that the smoker stands upright.

A caution

Do NOT empty the smoker on the site where one has been working as the fuel can easily ignite and start a fire on the site.

Because the beekeeper utilizes smoke and has to light his smoker, he is seen as a major fire threat to the farmer and in forestry areas. For this reason these folk are hesitant to welcome beekeepers or their unsupervised staff from placing bees on their farms. Therefore remember to always act responsibly when igniting and working with smokers.

"For so work the honey-bees, creatures that by a rule in nature teach the act of order to a peopled kingdom."

William Shakespeare

9 Observing bees at work

Let's imagine a swarm of bees has arrived and has moved into your dustbin or a box or drum in your yard in an undesirable place where the flying workers are going to present a problem for you. That same night well after dark and after the bees have settled for the first night, gently pick up the container and move it to a location at your premises where they can work undisturbed and where you will be able to work on them and enjoy them.

You have now received a great gift from God, praise the Lord. A whole new world has been opened to you, perhaps a hobby, or a small business to add to the plot's income or even to a much greater enterprise that you have never in your life envisaged. All leading commercial beekeeper undertakings started this way. You are now entitled to call yourself an apiarist to get away from the common term "beekeeper".

This new arrival swarm, because they have nothing to defend, are usually quite docile so sit yourself down on a comfortable stool to one side of the flight path and watch the goings on at the entrance of the bees' new home. If you feel more comfortable wear a veil but at this stage it should not be necessary. Now you have already learnt one thing and that is that bees have a flight work path and to walk across this path could involve a slight accident of a bee bumping into you.

On the first day you will notice large lazy zooming bees flying about. They are the drones, the male bees, and there will not be many of them. The other busy bodies are barren females. They are the workers and they are busy cleaning out their new home. They will be seen carrying out small bits of debris and quite amusing to see them dragging out a long thread of spider's web. Any dead bodies or foreign matter must go, and so they work away all day. Some are bringing in water to cool the home by evaporation and fanning with their wings at the entrance.

Other females in the home have formed their work curtain by hanging and linking their legs together to set the module for the cell sizes and, using wax produced from their bodies, have started building combs from honey brought with them from their previous abode.

On the second day after their arrival, the queen, the only producing member of the colony will start her main task of laying eggs and after a further three days there will be small bee grubs to feed.

Look carefully at the workers as they enter their home and you will notice small grains of pollen on their hind legs – this is their protein. The nectar brought in by the heavier landing bees, as they come crashing down at the entrance, is stored in the new cells and converted into honey, their carbohydrate. The nurse bees resident in the home devour these two ingredients and by regurgitating the residue they form royal jelly which is fed to the little bee grubbies for the first three days of their lives.

Where to from here?

Firstly, purchase a good quality bee veil, a pair of white overalls two sizes larger than you would normally wear, a pair of long socks, good leather boots with ankle supports as one sees in army boots (gum boots are a no-no). Add to this a good quality smoker and a hive tool (homemade hive tools are out!). Acquire a book called "Beekeeping in South Africa", known to beekeepers as the "blue book." All these items are obtainable from a stockist of beekeeping equipment[3].

Most important of all, join your local beekeepers' association where you will meet other beekeepers who will help and guide you along the way. Most associations present bee courses as beekeeping cannot be learnt only from books, but rather from hands-on mentorship, and the variety of programs presented at the monthly meetings also provides valuable guidance and tuition.

---

[3] I use Highveld Honey Farms, 185 Uys street Rynfield, Benoni.

<u>Notes</u>

""O bees, sweet bees!" I said;
"that nearest field is shining white with fragrant immortelles
Fly swiftly there and drain those honey wells.""
Helen Hunt

10 Using a brood chamber

By now a month has elapsed since that new swarm moved into our dustbin, which we had then placed under the trees in the far corner of the garden about three meters from the back wall. The worker bee grubs' cells were capped after eight days and after twenty three days the first cycle of new young workers hatched and the queen has already laid her second cycle and so these breeding cycles happen every twenty three days.

Without further delay this swarm must be transferred into a standard Langstroth brood chamber. This is a deep chamber into which is fitted ten brood frames properly nailed and wired with four tensioned horizontal high tensile stainless steel thin wires. The loose floor must be screwed to the bottom of the brood chamber. The lid comprises an inner flat lid over which is placed a telescopic lid. All the woodwork excluding the frames must be treated with hot, near boiling wax oil or creosote and left to dry for at least a month before the bees are introduced.

Insert a 20mm strip of foundation beeswax into the grooves of the top bars of the frames, then pour molten beeswax into the grooves to secure the strip of foundation. All of this equipment including all specially treated nails is obtainable from the suppliers of beekeeping equipment.

Our next item of equipment needed for the transfer is the smoker and a hive tool. The smoker is the only device the beekeeper has to combat and calm the bees.

Purchase these items, as homemade items are usually not successful. Dry pine needles make good smoker fuel, set alight and jammed tightly into the fuel barrel of the smoker. A cool white to light gray smoke is desired. Brown smoke is an indication that the smoker is choked and is dying out, and blue smoke is hot smoke – which is an indication of flames in the smoker barrel. This hot smoke burns and kills bees and brood must be avoided at all costs.

Before you begin, take a trip to the loo as there is nothing worse than a desperate nature call in the middle of a bee removal undertaking!

Next step is to check that you are properly dressed:

Use only a good quality bee veil - homemade veils are out. Starting from your skin outwards, vest and underpants first, cotton shirt next, a sweat absorbing tee shirt next, then thick jeans.

On goes the veil properly tied and then a white, clean, good quality overall made from thick material and zipped up the front is the last covering. Ensure that the veil is covered by the overall especially around the back of the neck and over the shoulders.

The overall must be tucked into long socks and the boots fitted. This dress gives the beginner all the confidence he needs as, although rather hot, the bees cannot get to him and sting him.

Let's proceed with the transfer...

You need a 20 litre drum and a large plastic bowl – each with a good fitting lid.

Onto each wired frame place three elastic bands – for the time being at one side of the frame. These elastic bands are to secure the combs as we cut them out of the swarm nest. Place the brood box, the 20 litre drum and the plastic bowl within easy reach of the work position.

Remove the frames out of the brood chamber and stand them externally next to the brood chamber.

Light the smoker and get it working properly.

Gently and with slow movement of your arms and body blow smoke all around the dust bin. Gently blow the smoke at the opening where the bees are entering the bin, and with the hive tool gently prize open the lid of the dustbin to ensure that the lid is loose all around. Apply smoke gently all around the openings of the loosened lid. Lift the lid and gently but firmly shake the bees into the brood chamber. Try to avoid any of the combs from breaking away and falling into the brood chamber.

Place the lid upside down on the ground in front of the dust bin. There is a 95% chance that the nest will be attached to the lid. Now get down onto your knees. Those strap-on knee pads are essential to save the material of the knees of your nice clean overall. Occasionally during the operation, one might need to smoke around gently to calm the bees.

Place the first frame horizontally over the brood box, and with the hive tool gently cut away the first comb where it is attached to the lid. Place this comb with the top of the comb tight up to the underside of the top bar of the frame and draw across the three elastic bands to hold the comb against the wires of the frame. Place this frame into the brood box against the side as this is the first frame. In the same way secure all the rest of the combs from the nest in the same sequence as they are removed and placed in the brood box.

Any damaged brood combs can be placed into the 20 litre drum and later thrown away and any unsuitable honey that perhaps breaks away or any capped honey can be placed into the plastic bowl for consumption.

Place first the inner lid and the outer lid onto the brood chamber and place the brood chamber in place of the dustbin with its entrance in the same direction as the previously observed work flight of the workers. Thump the dustbin down in front of the brood chamber and remove to the opposite side of the yard well away of the swarm.

Job complete and well done!!!

"Listen! O, listen!
Here come the hum the golden bees
Underneath full blossomed trees,
At once with glowing fruit and flowers crowned."
James Russell Lowell

11 Adding a super chamber

Our "dustbin hive", by now settled in its own brood chamber, will have hopefully gathered enough stores from the cosmos and blackjack flow to carry it well into the winter.

If this is a fairly strong swarm, the bees will have packed the three outer frames on each side of the brood chamber solid with honey and the brood nest will be on the remaining four frames in the centre of the brood chamber.

However if this is a medium to weak swarm the bees will need a little tender care over the cold months of June and July. It would be good to cover the hive with some sacking or canvas – but not plastic as this causes the hive to sweat on warm winter days.

Should one need to feed this swarm use an old plastic bottle and mix in equal volumes of white sugar and water. Remove two outer brood frames and stand this bottle in the back corner of the brood chamber right way up. Fill the bottle to the brim and tighten the lid firmly. With a needle prick a very small hole at the bottom side of the bottle so that the liquid forms just a drop on the outside surface of the bottle. Should the liquid run out freely, the hole is too large.

This bottle of sugar juice will last about a week but the bees will only take the sugar water as they need it and should there be sugar juice not taken and the small hole is clear then the bees will have sufficient food.

The month of May heralds the onset of the Highveld winter, with frosty nights and veld fires so therefore cut tall grass around the hive to ground level. Heat outside the hive causes the wax to melt and perhaps leak out at the hive entrance. Wax is highly inflammable and can set up a burning of the entire hive. But, the month of May is not for dreaming and admiring the beauty of our precious gums, it is a time for preparing for the oncoming Spring, which can be early as the end of July.

Eucalyptus Sideroxylon, better known as "black iron bark" is of the gum family and is winter flowering. It bears large beautiful cream, white, yellow, pink and red pom-pom type flowers and flowers from April until August, but only yields nectar on warmer days. However Eucalyptus Robusta, better known as the "brak gum", is the all winter favorite. It is, as the name implies, a robust gum tree with large wide tough leaves, gray bark, and large cream flowers. It yields both nectar and pollen and is relished by the bees. They work the flowers until late on winter days and into early evenings, often caught by the rapid onset of the cold night. They have been seen spending the night on the flower only to return to the hive the next day after the day warms up and they can fly again.

A honey producing chamber, known as a super chamber or just "super" will be required. These units are available at beekeeper supplier shops. Fit the open tongues before nailing the box and make sure that the finger grips are to the outside and that the rebate to carry the frames is at the tops of both the opposite sides. Use 63mm cement-coated nails obtained from the beekeeper suppliers.

To treat the super, dip it in boiling wax oil and leave it out in the sun to mature for about two weeks. Into the top rebates nail nine frame spacers, as we only use nine frames to the super and not ten. "Why?", you might ask. Because we get more honey from nine frames than we get from ten!

Next purchase precut shallow super frames, and 32mm cement coated nails. Nail the frames, two down through the top bar down into the side cheeks. Turn the frame, top bar downwards and nail the bottom bar downwards into the bottom of the side cheeks. Feed the stainless steel wire through the eyelets that should be facing outwards on the side cheeks and secure with small wiring nails to the side cheeks.

<u>Notes</u>

"The wild Bee reels from bough to bough
With his furry coat and his gauzy wing,
Now in a lily cup, and now
Setting a jacinth bell a-swing,
In his wandering."
Oscar Wilde

12 Buying a swarm

Bees are offered for sale in containers of mixed sorts, such as cardboard boxes, wooden boxes, small metal drums, or on standard frames where they have been caught as trek swarms by beekeepers who just wish to dispose of them. These are fine if on standard Langstroth frames and can be easily transferred into brood chambers.

Beekeepers who specialize in bee removals offer such swarms sometimes in exchange for a similar box with frames as they always have the problem that they are short of frames and boxes. Therefore one can prepare a suitable box with 5 to 8 frames, latch onto such a beekeeper, keep him supplied with boxes and he will keep you supplied with swarms. One can expect to pay about R20 for such a swarm exchange deal.

Bees offered for sale in receptacles without frames are not worth purchasing. In fact anyone having bees in such containers should expect that the beekeeper should charge to call and collect such a swarm and take it away. Such a charge would be about R100[4] or at least the cost of the petrol to fetch the swarm and place it in an apiary to be transferred to a standard brood chamber when time permits.

Bees in standard Langstroth hives are often advertised in farming magazines, and often with a super of honey. Prices for such hives range from R350 to R700 and if with a solid super of honey worth R200, at R700 is not a bad buy, considering that a new hive costs R750 without bees and honey.

Bees in an apiary of say 25 hives or more can sometimes be negotiated to include the standing place. Where one purchases say, 150 hives, the chances of negotiating the apiary sites are stronger as these bees are usually on farms and the farmer just needs to be notified that the bees are under new ownership. The trick is for the selling beekeeper to introduce the buyer to the farmer as someone who is his "assistant" and who will be visiting the apiary in his place.

Where 600 hives are sold which, at R400 each could cost the buyer R240,000, a deposit and terms can be arranged. This entire negotiated contract should run over two seasons. The apiary sites are taken over and a seller with 600 hives will have been a migrating beekeeper and the sites to where the beekeeper had been migrating should also be taken over.

The problem is that the hives, at this price, are sold as productive hives and the buyer needs to be satisfied that

---

[4] Every effort has been made to make illustrative costs and yields and other estimates as accurate as possible for 2012. The exchange rate of US Dollar to South African Rand was 1:7.74 on 28 April 2012.

they are in fact good producing hives. The buyer should number the hives and arrange to take over the hives, using the funds generated from the honey sold from these hives. In this way he is assured that he has purchased a productive swarm. He keeps a register of the number of each hive taken over with each payment that he makes. He could arrange to take them over in batches of 30's or 50's as his cash flow permits.

If, among these hives, there are empty, neglected and wax moth riddled hives complete with a super, the buyer needs to negotiate these hives at a much lower price according to their condition, say R100 each as some of these hives can be in very poor condition.

<u>Notes</u>

"The happiness of the bee and the dolphin is to exist.
For man it is to know that and to wonder at it."
Jacques Yves Cousteau

13 Catch swarms

Catch swarms are swarms that have voluntarily moved into a catch box. One will notice at first the "clean up bees " working around the catch box for some time, perhaps a week or two before the swarm is due to arrive. On the day of the swarm's arrival these "clean up bees" are no longer about, a clear indication that the swarm is about to arrive. Then with a mighty whirl the swarm arrives. They fly in and settle on the chosen box.

The bees will be seen sitting on the landing in front of the entrance of the box fanning a draught over their nosinov glands to beckon the rest of the swarm to the entrance where the queen had gone into the box. This is a sure sign that the queen is inside the box and a feature that the beekeeper should look out for.

Only move the box if one is positively forced to do so. The frames in the box are loose and bump around and with the slightest movement will injure bees – many of whom could be sitting between the frame end bars, or side cheeks and, worst of all, and the queen could be injured and die. As there is no brood in the hive as yet, the bees do not have an egg to draw a queen cell and all is lost. Laying worker occurs and the swarm dies away slowly.

The cleaning process starts immediately and the bees will be seen carrying out bits of debris and unwanted rubbish. Comb building starts right away with the honey in the bees' bodies carried over from the old hive. By the following day a piece of comb will have been built and eggs laid within 24 hours. The bees are very aware of the danger of loose frames in the hive and immediately start sealing up these loose parts with propolis.

The unit is best left alone for about a month. One will notice pollen being carried into the hive, which is a sure indication that brood rearing is under way. Bees not taking in pollen are taking in nectar or water. However, after two weeks, and armed with a little smoke, gently open the hive for a first peep to see what is happening.

Items to be checked

Cross building from one top bar into the next frame wiring. To correct this, cut the comb at the point where it crosses over and separate the two frames with a frame of a half or full sheet of wax foundation.

Check the brood pattern. A solid area of brood pattern is desired. Where this pattern is a scattered pattern, it is the sign of an old and failing queen. Should one discover queen cells under construction, leave alone – the bees know what they are doing.

Remove all frames containing strip catch box foundation and replace with frames of full or half sheets of foundation wax.

Catch swarms are very much "hit and miss" swarms. They can have old queens or young queens. If there are good brood patterns, place a queen excluder over the brood and give them a super with full foundation in all the frames or, better still, drawn comb super frames to encourage the bees to work into the super. Some literature advocates that one should kill the queen of a catch swarm to ensure a new queen who can be recorded and tracked during her active laying life. But my contention is that if the patterns are good, rather accept the situation and maybe kill the following year.

If the catch box with the swarm is in an undesirable position, then after three weeks move it away about 3 kilometers and return to its desired position after about a further three weeks and then do the inspections as set out above.

Migrating swarms occur practically throughout the year, depending upon the areas under review:

During spring time   (September to November), swarming occurs mainly in the eucalyptus areas of the Highveld and eastern Highveld;

During midsummer   (January to March), swarming occurs in the sunflower growing areas of Standerton and the eastern Free State;

During autumn (March to May), swarming occurs in the aloe growing areas north of Pretoria to Tzaneen, and in the eucalyptus grandis growing areas of Piet Retief, and below the eastern escarpment, Melmoth and Nongoma.

Virtually anywhere and anytime where bees are driven out by autumn grass fires, these swarms do not settle well and the queens are to be confined to their catch boxes once they have been caught. There are queen guards available to place over catch box entrances. These need to be regularly checked and cleared as the drones will block the queen guards and the workers will not be able to fly.

Where a swarm is caught in a standard brood chamber place a queen excluder between the floor board and the underside of the brood chamber to confine the queen in the new box for about one week after which time the queen excluder must be removed as the drones are also captured and die.

"What is not good for the swarm, is not good for the bee."
Marcus Aurelius

14 Catch boxes

Virtually any container can be utilized as a catch box or catching receptacle as long as it can hold standard brood frames. However let's deal with a few units for catching bees.

An old box is best suited because it has the aroma of a beehive, given off by the wax and propolis in the box and is fitted with 10 brood frames. Scout bees cannot resist such a box. The disadvantage is that the box is heavy and difficult to take down a ladder by oneself and one often needs an assistant. It is good to fit a strap or wire handle to enable one to carry the box with one hand whilst holding onto the ladder with the other, which makes the taking down task a little easier.

A new brood box is not successful and needs additional baiting to attract scout bees. The inside of the box must be treated by brush with a solution of propolis and mineral turpentine. The top bars of new frames also need to be coated. Good bait is to lay a 100mm x 100mm piece of foundation wax on the top outside of the lid at the entrance side of the box. Let the sun bake this onto the lid making it a permanent fixture.

The frames must be fitted with wires and a 15mm strip of foundation set into the groove of the top bars as starters for the bees. This is to avoid cross building of the new combs from one top bar to the other. This is done to avoid an unwanted disarray of comb building where side cheeks of frames do not touch one another and the important bee space is not provided.

Place the box on the lower edge of a flat roof facing away from the roof. Do not place the box in a difficult position for taking down one day.

Bees are easier caught where the box is a metre to three meters off the ground. Urban folk who intend to keep the swarm in their back yard should stand the catch box on a drum or temporary stand at the place where one eventually intends to keep the hive.

Nucleus boxes are narrow light wooden boxes. They should be fitted with a handle to enable one to remove them with one hand when climbing up or down a ladder. They hold five brood size frames and are also fitted with 20mm wide strips of foundation wax into the top bar groove. The five frames are best wired together to secure them to prevent the frames from bumping about which will injure the bees when the boxes are moved.

Small green boxes especially designed for catching bees also hold five brood frames, and are available to purchase from bee equipment suppliers. The frames must be wired together, the box closed and hung in a tree (hang four metres high to beat vandals). Use an extension or long ladder and secure the box against the trunk of the tree or in the fork of the branches. The idea being that the box must not wave about in the wind.

Tales of an African Beekeeper

Other receptacles are cardboard boxes, small drums, or apple boxes. Where such devices are used, they should hold a minimum of five brood frames and can be fitted with a wire sling handle. Due to their lightness, this means that they can be easily hung up in a tree or fitted somewhere on the scaffold branches of a tree.

Whatever one uses, it is important to hang or stand the device slightly falling forward but as level as possible across the frames to avoid cross building of the combs. The bees build their combs directly vertical and sideways sloping will cause the bees to build to the bottom of the next adjacent frame.

After the swarm has moved into the box, leave the unit undisturbed for about three weeks to allow the bees to wax or propolize the frames together. If one moves the newly caught swarm too soon, the frames rattle about and bees become squashed and killed. The queen could be killed or injured in this way and the swarm will die out queenless.

After about three weeks it should be possible to take the box down. Smoke the box, loosen the securing ties and gently carry down the ladder. Here too, some kind of handle or hook device attached to the box, makes this operation that much easier. Should you start this operation at about 3.00pm, hang the box at a lower level to allow all the confused returning field bees to settle before removing to another site at least 3 kilometers away.

<u>Notes</u>

"The little bee returns with evening's gloom,
To join her comrades in the braided hive,
Where, housed beside their might honey-comb,
They dream their polity shall long survive."
Charles Tennyson Turner

15 Swarms and swarming

As one drives around the smallholding areas throughout South Africa, one notices a beehive here or there – sometimes two or three together, owned by folk who know very little about bees and their habits. Their knowledge is limited to keeping a swarm, taking off honey when needed, extracting it in some primitive way, and then bottling it in a clean and presentable way fit for the table. Bees are temperamental creatures and these folk do not realize that they are playing with fire on a confined area such as a smallholding.

However, our focus is on the smallholder who does *not* wish to keep bees and having to deal with a swarm which flies into the feed room or outside store room.

Firstly, each and every smallholder should have beekeeping equipment so that he can don his kit and get in among the bees. Such equipment should comprise a white zip-up overall, a bee veil and a pair of beekeeping gloves. A bee smoker is the most essential item as this is his only weapon to drive away the bees. This kit of bare essentials would cost about R600, and is money well spent. Store this equipment together in a cupboard and the day will come when it will be called upon.

Secondly, one needs to know the habits of the swarming bees. Bees swarm for various reasons. There are two swarming situations, known as forced swarming and natural swarming.

Natural swarming

Natural swarming is where nature desires to multiply the species and a new swarm hives off from a parent swarm. Forced swarming can produce aggressive swarms whereas natural swarms are generally non-aggressive.

In the case of natural swarming, one will notice bees examining a location where they desire to set up home. For example, let us look at a cupboard in a workshop. They start buzzing around the cupboard, one or two at first and after a further two days or so there are now ten or up to twenty examining this location. These are scout bees and a sure indication that a swarm is coming. This scouting can go on for a week so there is plenty of time to take action. Spray the cupboard with Jeyes fluid or a carbolic acid solution made from Lifebuoy soap and water. Household insecticides like Doom are not successful as the odour dissipates too rapidly. One needs a solution that retains the odour for a few days. This action will chase the scouts so no further risk of the oncoming swarm.

A smoldering old rag left in front of the cupboard is sufficient, but no one wants to be gassed out of their own workshop by such an unpleasant smoke situation. Rags are also apt to flame so the risk of a fire is very real and is therefore not a good idea.

Forced swarming

Forced swarming is when a swarm is driven away from its abode as in the case of fire or flooding (if they were located in a hole in the ground), or by someone smoking them out of a location.

The forced swarm is the problem. They arrive unannounced and with no warning. They are usually hungry bees who have perhaps been on the move for a couple of days. They want to settle and get on with gathering stores and food as soon as possible and can be quite aggressive. So, what does one do?

Allow them to settle in the cupboard. After they settle and before they start working, simply move them. They are still in a travelling mode and will be none the wiser of the move. If it is possible remove the cupboard immediately to outside the store. This action does not allow the bees to orientate themselves to being inside the store. Once they start orientating to the store, they cannot be moved around on the plot. They become wandering lost souls, flying aimlessly all around looking for their cupboard, and they can become a real menace.

If they cannot be moved, contact the nearest beekeepers' association for the name of a beekeeper to come and remove them. However, if you have the equipment, light the smoker to burn dried leaves or dry thick grass, and gently scoop the bees into a cardboard box and stand the box outside the store. All flying bees will find the box and move into this abode.

Do not blow smoke onto the bees! But one can smoke the store to drive the bees out of the store so that they will fly to the cupboard now standing somewhere outside the store, or the cardboard box into which one has scooped the bees.

What you should NEVER do:

- Try to spray them with household insecticides;

- Try to burn them;

- Try to poison them;

- Try to wash them away with a strong jet of water;

- Try to kill them.

The bees will fight back, and a swarm on a killing rampage will tackle and kill every warm-blooded creature on the plot, and possibly the same on the adjoining plot.

What you should ALWAYS do

- Unleash any tethered animals such as dogs etc.;

- Put all children inside the house;

- Always work late afternoon so that if bees become aggressive you can be saved by the darkness.

What to do when stung

Retreat and cease operations immediately if one gets only one sting. Proper protection against stings such as kit and clothing is most important.

See Chapter 7 for more information on Stings.

Tales of an African Beekeeper

The Tale of the 'Knight in Shining Armour'

At a certain Parent-Teachers Meeting of Germiston High School, the principal announced that the swarm of bees living in the outbuilding premises had to be removed as they were occasionally stinging the groundsmen and were a threat to the children.

A quotation was solicited from a beekeeper, but it was considered to be too expensive and so was turned down by the meeting. After all, the beekeeper was getting a swarm of bees *and* the honey and he even had the audacity to charge! No, this was not acceptable and a young male from the knighthood of the parents offered to do the job free of charge if someone knew a beekeeper from whom he could borrow kit. Simultaneously he had the opportunity to show off his bravery to the young, attractive, single lady teachers of the staff.

At 11.00am on a hot summer's morning the young newcomer arrived at the scene all kitted up – overalls, bee veil, ladder and smoker puffing large volumes of smoke.

The children were warned to keep indoors and the ground staff took cover. In full view of the principal and some of the staff our young knight set up the ladder and clambered onto the flat roof to take on single-handedly the 'African Killer Bees that terrorise Argentina, Mexico, the gulf of Mexico and the southern states of America'.

The moment he thumped the ladder against the roof, the guard bees were alerted, and as he trudged over to the chimney with smoker ablaze, they suspected something was different to previous days and needed investigation. About 300 guard bees met our fearless friend. They buzzed about his head as he fumbled to light the fumitabs to do the poisoning. He dropped the tabs down the chimney into the room below, which chased the ground staff out to take cover elsewhere.

This cruel attempt to poison our little ladies failed. The bees declared war and managed to get inside the assailant's veil where they proceeded to sting him in the face, and around his mouth and nose.

At this point, he decided to flee the war zone, but in his haste the ladder slipped and he fell to the ground. To the horror of the onlookers, he lay motionless on the ground. The school secretary 'phoned the paramedics. Fortunately by the time they arrived most of the bees had lost interest in him and only a few bees buzzed around. This enabled the paramedics to get to him, load him onto a stretcher, into the ambulance and off to hospital. He sustained a broken ankle and broken arm and lived to tell the tale.

"My son, eat honey, for it is good, and the drippings of the honeycomb are sweet to your taste."

Proverbs 24:13, ESV

16 Beekeepers at your service

A beekeeper provides a service just as any other service provider – plumber, electrician, or motor mechanic. The beekeeper provides a bee removal service to the public and it is chargeable.

There are various ways of removing bees, each virtually peculiar to each circumstance. Only by experience does one become good at the work, realize how long the operation will take, and how many times one will need to visit the site to complete the job.

Advertising the service

To start, one needs to advertise in the local newspapers that circulate in the areas where one wishes to operate, along these lines:

"Bee removal service to sort out your bee problems. Please phone Mr. Beekeeper at number ..." Or,

"Bee problems?   Contact your local beekeeper for advice and a free quote to deal with the bees. Please phone ...."

It is also important to leave one's name and contact number with the municipality, the meter readers, the parks department and the fire department as these are folk who are frequently contacted by the public with bee problems.

Another option is to hand out leaflets to passing motorists, leave flyers at nurseries, or deposit flyers in street letter-boxes.

Answering 'the call'

Someone calls and where to from here?

Firstly, return the call as soon as possible as it may be a passing swarm settled in a tree or at the front door. State that you charge for the removal - do not go there first and then state that you charge.

Secondly, if the caller then elects to employ you, go out and give a quote and your conditions of payment. State what is involved and how long the job will take and to what extent the client will be inconvenienced. State that the charge is payable 50% on arrival and the balance on completion. Usually one can read the integrity of the client and if doubtful state that the fee is payable on commencement.

Thirdly, if given the go ahead then set about the task. Consider all the equipment necessary and tell the client that you will be back the next day to start. This gives the client the opportunity to get his act together and have his money ready for you.

Fourthly, execute and complete the work as professionally as possible. In this way you build up a good name and your name will soon be passed on by your client in their circle of friends. If you have small leaflets, leave a few with your client.

What to charge

The question always arises as to how much to charge. Based on a rate of R80.00 an hour and R2.00 per kilometer can one calculate a charge[5]. One must bear in mind that beekeepers are rare and not as common as plumbers and electricians and with confidence one can charge rates comparable to those asked by these service providers. One must take a professional approach to one's job and to the client when the occasion arises.

What to charge? This one learns by experience, but a few guidelines are as follows[6]:

A simple call out for a passing swarm hanging in a tree: R 50.00. This is a mere petrol reimbursement charge. Passing swarms usually move between 2.00pm and 4.00pm, therefore phone the caller first at about 5.00pm before setting out to confirm that the swarm is still there.

A meter box removal: R240.00. This is about an hour's job, but the box has to be left overnight to attract all the bees and can only be removed the following day. All in all this is a three trip job, the first day to quote, the second to extract the swarm and the third to take the swarm away.

A container that can be loaded and taken away: R300.00. This is a two day operation, one trip to quote and assess the situation, and the second, to load and

---

[5] These are 2012 estimates for labour and travel within a 20km round trip from the beekeeper's home base.

[6] These rates vary from swarm to swarm, situation to situation, city to city.

remove. You will need to pay an assistant to help you with loading, so a good spare kit needs to be in your equipment box.

A chimney or similar structure: R1,500.00 plus. You will need to pay an assistant beekeeper. You will need scaffolding and it could be a 5-trip operation.

It is not the beekeeper's job to make good any damage to the structure of the dwelling such as replacing ceilings etc. and the client must be made aware of all these factors.

Do not attempt a removal job that seems beyond your abilities. Eat humble pie and tell your client that the work is beyond your ability.

DO NOT TAKE ON A JOB THAT YOU CANNOT FINISH.

Perhaps you can call in a beekeeper to assist you or let him take charge and you assist him. Perhaps he will need to review the quote so that you too can be paid something to cover your costs. In this way you gain experience and next time you may be able to tackle the job and use someone else as your assistant.

Always leave your client happy with your services and you will build up a good name and a good living.

Tales of an African Beekeeper

A Tale: That's my honey!

Our neighbor of 40 years' standing received a swarm of bees in the chimney of their somewhat flat-roofed house. Bees in such situations are usually easily removed, however, the youngest son decided that the honey should be for them and not for the next-door beekeeper. They were warned not to allow the swarm to develop, as it was easy to remove them at this early stage. But the youngster decided that the longer they stayed the more honey they would eventually have for themselves and so the bees stayed for a year.

As in most cases with honey to guard, the bees started to sting the gardener whenever he set about to cut the lawns, so mother ordered the removal of the bees. The youngster decided that he would take on the job and kitted out with some borrowed equipment, and armed with a blazing smoker and a large bucket, he prepared to reach down the chimney and remove the honey by the handful into the bucket.

The bees were brought under control with the smoker and working at night there was not much resistance. As the robber carried out his task damaged combs fell down the chimney to the floor below, and honey was spilt on the outside of the chimney and on the roof. After about two hours the robber could not reach down any further into the chimney and so work ceased – he being rather disappointed as there was only a few handfuls of mixed honey, dead bees and wax in his bucket. Most of the combs were jammed somewhere lower down the chimney.

The next day the robbing bees from the neighborhood found the spilled honey on the roof and they took command. The neighbors spent the day indoors, the staff were sent home and the bees ruled the roost. By this time, mother's patience ran out and the youngster was summoned to remove the bees forthwith.

Now the fireplace in the elegantly furnished lounge had been removed and the opening boarded closed. However, damaged honey combs that had fallen down the chimney started leaking honey which dribbled under the boarding of the sealed up fireplace and into the lounge carpet. Soon, the little black sugar ants were there in their droves to get their fill of the spoils. At this point the boarding was removed to see what was happening – and immediately bees came crawling and flying into the lounge.

Now our youngster had to find a quick fix solution to please mother. So, kitted out in broad daylight hours, he climbed onto the roof and decided to poison the bees by pouring three or four cupfuls of petrol down the chimney. Some knowledgeable pal had told him that petrol kills bees instantaneously and so this was his quick fix solution.

From the rooftop he yelled, "Never mind Ma, soon our troubles will be over!"

Now the bees' tempers were being frayed and they started to take revenge on him. The smoker began to work overtime as he vigorously pumped the bellows of the smoker down into the chimney. Before long a flame escaped into the chimney... this was all the petrol fumes needed and within seconds there was an almighty explosion.

Tales of an African Beekeeper

Well, the fireplace opening into the elegantly furnished lounge was the line of least resistance and all the muck, old black combs, dead bees and honey burst into and across the lounge. The opposite wall, from the ceiling to the floor, was soon 'decorated' with this sticky muck and debris.

The tale ends with the neighbors repainting the entire lounge, laying a new wall-to-wall carpet, reupholstering some of the soft furnishings and buying new curtains.

Next time call a beekeeper.

<u>NOTES</u>

"The bee is more honoured than other animals;
not because she labours, but because she labours for others."
Saint John Chrysotom

17 Poisons and Repellents

Generally bees are sensitive to most poisons – even those pesticides that are marked "bee friendly" can be toxic to bees. Micro encapsulated pesticides are particularly risky because they kill only when ingested. The bees collect it with pollen and when the bees consume the pollen they die – sometimes weeks later, which makes it difficult to trace the poison that killed the bees. Be very careful when placing bees near citrus orchards. Most powdered insecticides used in fruit orchards and perhaps on bean lands have the same consequences.

Poisons

In extreme cases when bees are a danger to man or animals it is necessary to destroy the bees.

Phostoxin is the poison to do the job. It is a poison registered with the Department of Agriculture and is available at farm suppliers' outlets. It emits phoxotine gas which is very toxic to anything that breaths. It is also registered to control wax moth. Treated equipment can be reused after vented for 24 hours. Phostoxin is a slow worker with sometimes failing effectiveness.

Dichlorvos is not registered for the control of bees but is very effective and kills a swarm within minutes even in fairly open and exposed areas. It comes in liquid form and gives off a gas that will kill them. Do not use it on hive parts as the liquid penetrates the wood and the wax and is very difficult to remove. The gas has a very short effective period of approximately 5 hours. New swarms have been reported to have moved into a treated nest within two days.

Chlorpiriphos dissolves in water and is very effective in destroying bees in open nests, particularly if mixed with dichlorvos. Chlorpiriphos is a long acting poison and must not be used near any equipment that is to be reused.

Sunlight liquid soap or any other soapy solution mixed to a strong solution in water and sprayed over the bees will kill them by asphyxiation.

Repellents

Repellents are used to drive bees away from an area or to discourage bees from entering and occupying an area.

Carbolic acid. Bees dislike the smell of carbolic acid. Beekeepers have been known to fabricate a framed cloth board from maisonite or a multiply board. Cut a board to the size of a super chamber. Along the surround fix a 20mm x 15mm wood surround. Onto the surface of the board between the surrounds glue an absorbent cloth material. To this cloth scatter about two hundred drops of the carbolic solution. This board is placed over the honey super to drive the bees down and out of the super. Cavities treated with carbolic acid oil will also not be occupied by bees. However carbolic acid is very volatile and will evaporate very quickly.

Benzeldahide, also known as bitter almond oil, is also disliked by bees. They will abandon an area when fumes are blown over them.

Jeyes fluid and Sunlight liquid. A solution of Jeyes fluid and Sunlight liquid soap mixed with water and sprayed onto areas from where swarms have been removed will prevent a new swarm from taking over the vacated area. This repellent is only effective for about three months, which should give the beekeeper the opportunity to take other measures to prevent the bees from returning.

The smoker is the best tool to drive bees away from one area to another. It is easy to control both for directing and for intensity of the application of repellent required.

A Tale of Poisoning Gone Wrong

It's late one Monday morning when I answer the telephone and a young female voice rings out loud and clear,

> "This is Veshan's Bicycle Shop, Main Road, Benoni. Please come quick! The bees are stinging everyone in the street, and my husband has been taken to hospital. We know you are a beekeeper with some experience and we are sure you will be able to help us!"

To be sure, they must have done something nasty to our little ladies bearing the name of African Killer Bee, for them to have flexed their muscles. Certainly our bees will not stand for any cruel deeds inflicted upon them. They would then delight to send one or two perpetrators to hospital if they could.

There is not much one can do when bees are on the rampage other than just taking cover and keeping clear of the war zone, perhaps 300 meters away. But in answer to the distress call, better toddle along, take some heavy protective kit and show some concern as one is looked upon as highly experienced and able to wave the magic wand that will restore peace.

Arriving at the war zone, the street was cordoned off by some traffic officers about 50 meters on either side of the cycle shop. In the middle of the street stood a large red fire engine, lights flashing with two hoses leading into the cycle shop.

Picture an Indian bicycle shop in an old house that had been converted into a shop. Most of the internal walls had been removed and the roof was mainly supported by some magical 'skyhook'. Imagine and expect to see what one would find in a cycle shop. Rows of small colorful children's cycles and tricycles, rows of ladies and gents cycles, wheels and tyres hanging from the ceiling hooks, fishing rods and fishing gear, trays with cycle spares, nuts and small bolts in small trays, and what seems like hundreds of other gadgets.

To the side of the shop was an old chimney which had not been demolished, as there had always been a swarm of bees in that chimney. One estimates that these bees must have lived there for a good number of years, perhaps 10 years.

The two firemen at the end of the two hoses were trying their best to fight the bees. There was water flying in all directions and the larger of the two hoses was emitting a spontaneous spurt of white foam that missed the flying bees but splashed all over the walls, and the contents of the shop – what a mess!!! High up on the walls there were bees with wet wings, their backs stuck to the walls, their little bums wriggling about with only one thought in mind, "Just wait until our wings dry off and we are able to fly – we will be at you all over again!"

Upon further investigation the young lady who had sent out the earlier distress call revealed that on the Sunday night her brothers, husband and father had tried to poison the bees so that they could remove the honey from the chimney. They had spilled honey on the shop floor, down the sides of the chimney, outside on the roof, down the ladder and onto the pavement in front of the shop. Robber bees from other swarms in the vicinity had found the honey and that had started the fight among the bees. The bees also blamed the innocent folk in the street for the cruelty inflicted on them by the Indians who tried to poison them. So out went the message from our little darlings, "fight and kill any warm blooded creature that moves, and ask questions later."

Someone should have told Veshan's never to try to poison bees, but to call the experts first, not last!

<u>NOTES</u>

"Aerodynamically, the bumblebee shouldn't be able to fly, but the bumblebee doesn't know it, so it goes on flying anyway."
Mary Kay Ash

18 Working and controlling bees

By nature bees are not aggressive like some animals – survival is their primary object. The protection of their queen, their brood and their honey stocks depends directly on their survival and interference with any of these will definitely lead to stinging.

Secondly, interference with their environment, such as the ploughing of ground, grass-cutting or disturbing any other vegetation will aggravate them. Dust, smelly compost heaps and chicken runs, and wet, sweaty animals such as sheep and especially horses are to be avoided. In addition, the threat of an approaching storm and the presence of lightning sets the bees on edge and a stinging fight can result.

Using the Smoker

Smoke is the beekeeper's only weapon to calm and subdue bees. The bees, when smoked, immediately fear a fire that will burn down their nest, and so they immediately prepare to abandon the nest. They gorge themselves with honey. They are not aware of the presence of the beekeeper nor even the fact that their hive has been opened. They are only concerned with packing up and moving as soon as possible. And during this brief spell of about two minutes the beekeeper must open the hive. Once the hive has been opened and a frame or two taken out, the bees become demoralized and a little smoke blown around the open hive calms them immediately.

Only use good quality smoke. Cool white or light grey smoke is ideal. Blue smoke is hot smoke and once one notices blue smoke coming out of the smoker, the smoker must be attended to so as to provide the light smoke desired. Dry pine needles, dry blue gum leaves, dry grass and pieces of gum tree bark are good. Too much bark creates blue smoke and must be used in moderation although bark does keep the smoker going well. Old carpet underfelt also makes good smoker material.

Dry animal dung only aggravates the bees and must not be used. A good tip is to add one or two pieces of propolis to the smoker, which will gives the bees the real sensation that the nest is burning. It is also pleasing to the beekeeper that is also getting a good dose of smoke. Do not add wax to the smoker as this tends to block up the smoker nozzle.

Overworked smokers can emit a flame and can burn the bees. Should one need to blow smoke into the bee veil if bees are harassing the beekeeper's vision, be aware that the veil is made of synthetic fabric that can ignite and one could blow a large hole through the veil.

Wear clean white overalls for day work and denim blue for late afternoon and night work. Wear a garment under the overall to absorb perspiration because perspiration penetrating through the overall causes the overall to adhere to ones shoulders and underarms and at these points the bees sting through the overalls. These lodged stings render the overall to be dirty. The odour of the stings remains in the overall and immediately upsets the bees when the overall is used on another occasion.

Opening the Hives

The very first task before going to the hives is to light the smoker and make sure it is working well.

Approach the hive to be opened from the back. Smoke it well into both entrances and any other bee leaky openings, and wait for about a minute. Smoke again, and insert the hive tool under the lid and gently prize the lid open. Lift the lid about 30mm and smoke under the lid. Then remove the lid and knock the bees off with one sharp jolt on the ground in front of the hive.

If the hive has a super on it and one does not wish to look into the super, then insert the hive tool between the super and the brood chamber and lift both lid and super together. Place the super onto another board to keep closed. A great number of worker bees, trapped in the super, are immediately out of one's way. Gently smoke over the brood chamber, now remove the queen excluder if there is one and place it on edge next to and against the brood chamber. Briefly check to see whether the queen is perhaps walking under the queen excluder, If she is, gently allow her to go down into the brood chamber.

Gently with slow movements now over the open brood chamber, smoke the air again and remove the second frame from either side. At this stage one will notice the bees moving to one side of the brood chamber where the queen is to be located. Always remove the frame at the opposite side to which one notices this movement. Stand the frame vertically against the brood chamber and proceed to now remove the first frame. Now with two frames outside the brood chamber, there is sufficient space to move the other frames about without damaging bees.

Work slowly and with positive movements. Smoke only if the bees are flying excessively around one's head or hands. Avoid killing, squashing or injuring bees. With practice this is easily achieved.

Only open hives for a particular reason and now proceed to close again. Replace the frames in the same sequence as they were originally in the brood chamber. Replace the queen excluder and the super or just the lid if there is no super.

Understanding the Mood of the Bees

Bees have different moods for different seasons and different moods for different times of the day. So before one approaches a swarm, one can have a fair idea of what to expect, but it is also important to be able to recognize the mood of the bees.

In the very early Spring, the bees are usually hungry and short-tempered – perhaps caused by flowers secreting nectar on warm days and not the next day which is a cold day. The easiest time to work on hives is in the late afternoon in built up areas, and mid-afternoon in open farm areas. It is not good practice to open hives at this early spring time as the bees, because of the cold, find it difficult to seal up draughty cracks caused by opening the hive parts.

Tales of an African Beekeeper

Spring proper and early Summer (September, October, November) is a busy time for bees. They are content and working flat out and because of this very busy scenario, one can walk around the apiary unmolested, a sure indication that all is well. The bees want to get on with their job rather than concern themselves with the beekeeper, and so this is an easy time to open hives and work with bees. Under such conditions, one can do almost any manoeuvre with the swarm, such as re-queening, splitting swarms, uniting swarms, swapping field forces and any other experiments, without causing the swarm to abscond or be unduly disturbed.

Mid-Summer (December) is the turn of the seasons and an in-between time with a lull in the nectar flow as the midsummer and late summer flowers have not started flowering as yet. The bees are very short-tempered, searching everywhere for food and one can expect a lot of resistance. They greet the beekeeper before he even disembarks from his vehicle. No walking around the apiary on these days without interference from the bees, therefore be quick to don the veil and light the smoker. As this is the robbing time of the early honey crop, the best time to work is very late - as the sun is setting and into the early evening. This is the less risky time to open hives for fear of a major stinging spree, especially on hives kept on smallholdings. The beekeeper needs extra protection, such as two pairs of overalls over jeans and tracksuit top. Disturbing bees at this dearth period of December can cause them to abscond from their hives.

Mid-summer to early autumn (January, February, March) presents a host of flowering again. The bees become very busy again but unlike the spring flow, they do not accept too much interference and are apt to abscond. The theory is that they are preparing for the winter and undue disturbance of the swarm, such as opening brood chambers, causes them to move. One cannot walk around the apiary unprotected as in the spring even though the bees are very busy. Best time to rob is late afternoon into early evening and not later than the end of March.

Autumn and early winter (April, May) is the time when bees are preparing for the winter. They do not like being disturbed at this time and carry their disturbed condition into the following day. They will most certainly greet the beekeeper should he appear at the apiary again the following day. Best time to rob is very late and into the evening. Only surplus honey should be taken and sufficient left (at least five super frames) to carry the bees through the winter to spring or early August.

At all times after working on bees, do not leave any wasted honey traces around the hives. This causes robbing the following day, which in turn, causes fighting between the foraging bees and the swarms. The weaker swarms are liable to be attacked and robbed by the stronger swarms. The beekeeper is helpless to stop this rampage, as the bees do not respond to smoke and the best thing to do is to enter the apiary well-protected and place in a bucket any spilt honey still found lying around.

"How sweet are your words to my taste, sweeter than honey to my mouth!"

Psalm 199:103, TNIV

19 Avoid stressing bees

Bees are stressed under various circumstances that should be avoided as far as possible:

Incorrect placement of hives at apiary sites

- Standing in the full sun all day.

- Standing in full shade all day, especially on the south sides of buildings or plantations.

- Away from a water source. Water should be available within 300m of the hives.

- Facing south into the cold winter wind.

- In flooding areas or areas where drainage run-off will not occur.

- Entrances must be lower than backs of hives to allow moisture from condensation to run out of the hives.

- Over populating an apiary site.

- Too much weed growing around the hives especially in the workers' flight paths.

Foreign insects and other animals

- Fast run-about ants that continually harass the bees by running amongst the incoming bees on the landings of the hives.

- Small black sugar ants that usually enter and harass weak swarms.

- Toads that sit and catch the odd loaded bee at the hive entrances.

- Birds that continually catch the odd bee particularly the Fork Tail Dronger.

- Pirate bees that sit on the top of the hives and catch the odd loaded bee. Hives placed in deep shade can overcome this menace.

The beekeeper

- Unnecessary and frequent opening of hives. The bees seal the hive parts, such as broods to supers, and particularly in cold weather it takes a long time for the bees to reseal these areas.

- Over-robbing the swarm, especially if it is a very large swarm, as the bees need to consume honey as part of their daily diet and if insufficient honey is left the bees will starve and die out, or abscond.

- Unclean robbing, that is leaving pieces of honey comb lying about the apiary, which sets up robbing amongst the hives.

- Over smoking the bees with too hot smoke that burns the bees.

- Migrating too frequently. Two moves a year is safe but four times a year is too stressful and overworks the queen causing her to fail having worked only a short period.

The weather

- Too much space in the hive during very cold weather.

- Too large a hive space for a swarm to keep warm where a small swarm is hived.

- Long cold rainy spells can cause brood diseases.

- Continual wind, as experienced on the eastern highveld particularly between Springs and Ermelo.

- Continual very cold frosty nights.

- Flooding of the area where the bees are standing. Water rising up into the hives above the entrances causes the bees to suffocate, and brood diseases cause the swarm to abscond.

<u>NOTES</u>

"The air came laden with the fragrance it caught upon its way, and the bees, upborne upon its scented breath, hummed forth their drowsy satisfaction as they floated by."
Charles Dickens, The Curiosity Shop

20 Loading and moving bees

The moving of bees stresses the bees, and stressed bees cause various disorders in the colony, among which is the possibility of take-over of the colony by the "capensis invaders".

Moving bees may also cause the following disturbances:

1) The food and water supply is disrupted without warning to the bees, who are suddenly plunged into a situation of no water on the new site. Shortage of food is not as serious as the shortage of water.

2) The queen immediately stops producing and her laying cycle can take days to re-establish.

3) All internal functioning of the brood is disrupted.

Being well aware of the risks involved, the beekeeper who needs to move hives should do everything possible to minimize the stresses of the move.

Before the move

First, know exactly where you are going to off-load, even to the exact spots where the hives are going to stand. If the site is new to you, visit the site a day or so before and put out markers that you can follow in the night. Check closely for those "runabout long-legged" ants that must be avoided. Even if the site is not new, visit it the day before as things such as gates and fences could have changed since the last time you were there. If there is a guard at the entrance gates to your site area, advise him of your approximate arrival time.

Always tell someone exactly where you are going, and the time that you anticipate to be back at home-base. Always carry your cellphone along with you and preferably, DON'T GO ALONE.

Loading (closing down entrances)

Start loading about half an hour *after* sunset in the summer, and half an hour *before* sunset in the winter. Aim to be loaded and roped down before total darkness.

Gently smoke the hive entrance to chase the guards into the hive. If you have to smoke into the entrance, allow 10 seconds for the bees to expel the smoke and plug the entrance with a foam rubber plug. Midway across the back of the hive between the brood and the super, crack the hive with the hive tool and insert a match to create a permanent crack for the duration of the move.

There is some debate about whether or not to close the entrances...

If one does close down the entrances, the following happens:

1) The bees lack ventilation,

2) Panic is set up in the colony and unnecessary heat is generated as the bees attempt to find their way out,

3) Claustrophobia prevails and bees are as stressed as we humans.

If one *refrains* from closing the entrances the following happens:

1) The bees, including the queen, crawl out of the hive and walk up and settle on the front of the hive. If their hive is up against another hive in the transport, the bees crawl onto both hives and become separated when the hives are off loaded.

2) The workers become separated and many die on the transport loading surface. Especially in very windy and rain stormy weather the bees are blown off the hive and are lost.

Gently pick up the hive and place it on the transport loading surface. Do not drop or thump it down. Place the entrance facing to the back of the travelling direction and the frames parallel to the direction of travel. Place the hives alongside each other, and one can load one hive high upon one other hive. Rope down the hives and make sure that a hive cannot fall off the back of the truck. Drive with care to avoid jarring or thumping the hives on ridges, ruts or potholes in the road. This jarring about causes the honey combs in the frames to break and dribble honey down inside onto the floor of the hive. Bees drown in this honey, which induces them to leave the hive the very next day after offloading.

At the destination, gently offload the hives to the permanent positions where they will stand. Ensure that the hives slope to the entrances and that bees do not cross one another's work flight path when they will be working. Place each hive entrance at a different angle to the sun if possible. Avoid low lying hollows that can flood during a heavy storm or downpour. Allow the bees to settle and then remove all the foam plugs and the match spacer at the back of the brood chamber.

Moving during the day

Load as before, but at sunset the previous night. Place shade cloth nets over the load to close up all possible holes so as to contain any bees that could find their way out of the hives. Ride as early as possible to avoid the heat of the day and plan to be offloaded by 9 o'clock in the morning. Carry a good amount of water in cans along with the trip, so that, should one encounter delays that extend into the heat of the day, water can be sprinkled through a watering can over the hives to cool them off.

Moving bees a short distance (less than 3 kilometers)

In such cases, the hives entrances must be plugged up with dry grass which the bees will remove themselves over a period of 3 days.

Moving bees 10 meters on the standing site

Every third day over a period as long it would take, a hive can be moved 2.5metres backwards or forwards and half a meter left or right sideways.

Turning the direction of the entrance

This can be done every third day to an angle of 45 degrees.

The Tale of the Long Walk

The weather was terrible and after a midnight rainstorm the road we had used on the way in was very slippery on the way out. In fact it was so slippery that we ended up in the ditch. We had offloaded the bees so we had no stability, as compared to a fully laden truck. Unfortunately the land on which we got stuck was uninhabited land that the farmer had leased from the government. As a result we had to walk about two kilometers to the farmhouse. However, the farmer wasn't prepared to come out in that weather with his tractor because he would get stuck himself, so we decided we'd have to walk home.

But first we had to walk back to the truck and take out the battery. We were careful to hide the battery in the sunflower land, measuring out where we had hidden it, for collection in the morning. And then we set off for home – this was a 23km walk in the never-ending downpour. In our white kit, nobody was going to pick US up! We got home at 4am!

About five days later the farmer called to tell us that he had finally pulled our truck out of the ditch and we could come and fetch it. Of course, we first had to go and find our battery hidden on the sunflower lands, and everything looked quite different in the clear light of day. Anyway, we found it after much scratching around, and lived to beekeep another day.

"He said the pleasantest manner of spending a hot July day was lying from morning till evening on a bank of heath in the middle of the moors, with the bees humming dreamily about among the bloom, and the larks singing high up overhead, and the blue sky and bright sun shining steadily and cloudlessly."

Emily Bronte, Wuthering Heights

21 Country apiary sites

The Ideal site

- Frost free area. Light frosts are acceptable but heavy frosts need specially protected shelters, especially from the south winds.

- Generally good rainfall is desirable.

- Areas producing two flows such as gums and cosmos, or gums and sunflowers, or kidney beans are best.

- The nearer to home base the better.

- Farm sites are best as this enables one to work anytime during daylight hours.

Farm sites

When seeking a farm site always go alone. Farmers do not seem to like to be outnumbered at a first meeting.

In most cases the farmer will place you in an area of the farm to which he seldom goes. This is usually because the road to the area is problematical due to very uneven ground, or having to cross marshy areas that sometimes become very wet in rainy weather. These are "no go" areas so do not hesitate to turn them down. You can impress upon him that you will require his services to help you get out. These words always work and he will often propose an alternate site.

Once a site is agreed, remember the following:

- When entering an unknown area, always walk it first. Watch out for holes, rocks, tree stumps, wire and bits of steel that could damage your vehicle, nothing worse than to receive two punctures at the same time. More importantly, watch for muddy or slippery surfaces on seemingly hard minor farm roads.

- When first visiting and if the site is suitable, place markers so that you can find your way in at night. The terrain is completely different at night.

- Always leave the site on the same road that you went into the site area.

- During daytime visits to the farm, try to find another way into the site. Should a tree fall over your regular way in, you then have an alternate route.

- Always locate your hives exactly where the farmer showed you.

- Be wary of cattle camps where there are bulls. They are most unpredictable beasts (thank goodness they do not bite!)

Tales of an African Beekeeper

Good practices

Always remember that the farmer is the one who may have to haul you out of the mud at 10.00 o'clock at night, so maintain a good relationship with your farmer:

- Keep in close contact with your farmer by calling first before going to the farm.

- Always try to greet the farmer, and one or two bottles of honey does wonders – especially if it is honey from his own farm!

- Always close the gates even if you found them open. The rule is that the last man through the gate closes it.

- Should a farmer ask a favour always try to oblige. There are often bee problems on farms and always in the most awkward places. Try to help out but do not take on a job beyond your abilities. You could leave the farmer with more of a problem than the bees presented before you touched them.

- Always keep good relations and he will forward you to other farmers with a good reference.

Resting place after working

There is nothing better than a good resting place on a river bank under the willow trees with lunch and good liquid refreshment. So always carry a ground sheet (which is also useful for that good nap under the trees to round off the site visit). Use the time to change into dry clothing to keep one healthy and free of colds and flu.

A Tale from the African Bushveld

It was May and we set off to visit a farmer in the nature reserve where we had last been three years ago. Rains in the past two years had not been good, and our expectations for a honey crop were too low so therefore we had not been back. But the magnificent honey crop of three years ago beckoned us to return.

With ten bottles of honey in our basket, we arrived to surprise our farmer friend. He and his wife were overwhelmed to see us and with open arms, hugs and kisses, they greeted us with the warm love of true Christians. For us this seemed like a family home coming and in no time coffee and Ouma's rusks were set out on the stoep[7] for us.

The usual questions were asked, "Where have you been for the last two years? We missed you and thought you had seen the beekeeping joke and given up?" The usual reply is, "Well, we tried something else, but this is best for us, so here we are again."

Fortunately our notes gave us the children's names and to their surprise, we remembered their names and asked after them. We asked especially after daughter Anna, who had got married three years ago. They were amazed that we had remembered these facts and this further strengthened our "family ties". Eventually after many rounds of conversation and second cups of coffee we were told that we were very welcome to return to the previous site where we had stood before.

The farmer drove us up and over the hill to our previous site in the nature reserve, which had changed

---

[7] A patio, or porch.

as he had harnessed a natural spring in the hills and built a dam as he had invested in more game. He invited us to stay and utilize the lapa, the braai area and toilet facilities, and offered that we could camp there and stay over for a few days with our bees if we so wished. This we could not resist, so final plans were laid that we would arrive in July, set up camp, and then follow with the bees a day or two later. After more coffee and rusks we said our final good byes and returned to home base.

Eventually camp was set up and we had thirty swarms on site. The general bush looked like a million dollars and previous records were now running true and we were in for a bumper crop. We immediately set about the Spring cleaning, slept the night in our tent, cooked a whopping breakfast and returned to home base with all the brood honey and unwanted frames. We did not want to store this honey on the site which the bees would find and give us a robbing problem.

The bushveld, if one has not camped out there, has its hidden agendas. There are honey badgers, baboons, and puff adder snakes that like to bask in the sun during the day and crawl in under the hives at night for some warmth from the bees. There is the odd leopard in the hills that keeps the baboon populations down, and because there are not many wild swarms, the badgers are few and far between. The European bee eater and the Fork tailed Dronger birds are always about and are something of a menace. There are thousands of spiders, from small kite spiders to large colorful garden spiders, whose webs are strung between trees looking for their daily catch. The large rain spider, as big as a lady's hand will scuttle around the stones and tufts of grass looking for its daily bread. The shy spitting cobras seem to keep clear of any movement but the farmer warned us that they were about.

As time passed, we spent the odd overnight stay just marveling at the millions of stars in the cool, clear winter nights. The Scorpio constellation would be up in the eastern sky and the peace of God's creation was quite awe-inspiring.

By the end of August it was time to return to take off the aloe honey. The aloe flowering had been good and honey would be plentiful, so loaded with empty supers to exchange for full honey-loaded supers we set off to the reserve.

We had not been back to the site for about three weeks and when we arrived, the dull downward expression on the farmer's face suggested that all was not well. So it was with some trepidation that we bounced along on the jeep track road, over the hill and down to the hives.

The site was Dunkirk all over again. The honey badgers and the baboons had found and smashed every single hive. Broken debris was scattered all over the area where the hives had stood and not a drop of honey or a piece of brood or wax comb could be found. They had taken the lot, three hundred brood frames and two hundred and seven super frames had been written off plus about four hundred kilograms of aloe honey. We managed to recover all the floors and lids of most of the supers and about sixty percent of the brood boxes.

The honey badgers go for and eat the brood, and their powerful front claws rip through the sides of the brood boxes like matchwood. The bees are totally demoralized and swarm off to save their lives from the feasting of the birds. This leaves the baboons some easy pickings and the beekeeper has little choice but to write his experience off to the fact that this is Africa, and others who inhabit this peaceful garden of God, also have to live.

The farmer bade us farewell and invited us to return again one day – if only to camp in the bush and to try something else again with our bees.

<u>NOTES</u>

"The sky was of the deepest blue, with a few white, fleecy clouds drifting lazily across it, and the air was filled with the low drone of insects or with a sudden sharper note as bee or bluefly shot past with its quivering, long-drawn hum, like an insect tuning-fork."

Sir Arthur Conan Doyle, Beyond the City

22 Bee camps

Unfortunately bee camps are essential and cost money to build and maintain. Therefore one should look around for an area that is secure, near eucalyptus trees, has a gate and is able to be locked. All these requirements have to be achieved and some afternoon shade will be a bonus. To build a camp to house 24 hives will cost in the vicinity of R900.

These are some areas that one could investigate:

Farm camps

A small enclosed camp on a farm, perhaps somewhat neglected but needing slight repair is ideal. Any repair work done to his property is looked upon by most farmers in admiration, and will definitely count in your favor. The rent for the site is usually determined by payment in honey, the going rate is a bottle of honey per hive per year, either given all at once or in smaller amounts during the year when visiting the site.

If no such site is available then one would have to construct a camp on the farm at a spot designated by the farmer. Usually farmers usher one to a remote part of the farm that he does not use and these areas are usually across a marshy or rain flooding area. Therefore when negotiating an area always make sure that one has good access to the site in all weather conditions. Always advise the farmer of your intended coming and going on his farm.

Grave Yards

A remote corner in an enclosed graveyard is suitable. Modern graveyards are well fenced and gates are locked every night, so one usually has to obtain a key for after-hours access. If the area is used as a permanent site, then access can always be during daylight hours.

These areas are obtained from the municipal parks department. They are usually pleased to have contact with a beekeeper to call upon when they are in need of assistance with their bee problems. These sites are always negotiable and one can offer to assist them with minor bee problems at no cost to them. However, don't commit to major bee removals free of charge.

Old buildings

There are many derelict old buildings around old disused mine properties where roofs have been removed. A room area can be selected and a good security gate fixed in the opening. Old window openings can be bricked up to create only the single gate entrance. A board with one's name and telephone number must be displayed to notify anyone of the owner of the apiary.

Constructing camps

Camp construction will not be discussed in detail, as this must be to one's own design but one must use creosoted wooden poles. Steel poles rust at ground level and need constant painting and maintaining. The wire can be Bonnox type fencing or barbed wire and razor wire in the flat is best. Coiled razor is also good, laid slightly off the ground around the outside and secured to the Bonnox fencing from the inside of the camp.

Circular camps, no less than 20 meters in diameter, are easiest to construct. Beehives placed in circles and facing outwards eliminate a drifting problem in scutellata bees. Also to add to the security aspect, one can plant a hedge around the outside of the camp. Broad leaf privet planted at 300mm centres makes a good hedge in a short three-year period. A grape vine grown and entangled through the wires within three years will also make a good inaccessible hedge.

All these types of camps must be kept free of long grass and weeds, which present a fire hazard that can burn years of labor up in ten minutes.

Vandals always try to be that step ahead, and will find their way in through weak areas of the camp construction. One has to constantly visit the camps, about once a month, best at irregular times, and hoping that one is seen at the camp. Where vandals have entered the apiary camp site, one has to improve the weak spot to avoid a re-entry in the same way and area.

When seeking camps, whether on farms, or at municipalities, always go alone. Always meet your contact face to face; phone calls are a waste of time even if you know the person on the other side. Go with a small bucket or a bottle or two of honey.

<u>Notes</u>

*"How doth the little busy bee
Improve each shining hour,
And gather honey all the day
From every opening flower."*
Isaac Watts

23 The notebook

One of the most valuable items of equipment that the beekeeper can possess is his notebook of the comings and goings to his various sites over a period of years. The notes are continually referred to from one year to the next and improvements made on the previous year's shortcomings and mistakes, and so one grows an easy running business. The notes must be designed for easy reference without a lot of unnecessary padding.

First Section

This is the index and contains the names and telephone numbers of all folk relating to **sites**, such as farmers, municipal officials, parks directors, mine officials and everyone relating to sites.

A second section of the index contains **sales** information – the names of all folk to whom you sell honey and the prices charged as well as notes as to when prices are increased. The object of this section is to keep prices uniform, and to record increases at regular periods and the amounts thereof.

Thirdly, names, locations and sites of bee **removals**, because bees often return to old sites and these details will enable you to do your rounds and call on these sites again for another removal job and another swarm. (Remember to always leave a removal site with enough bait to attract another swarm). Always write the amount of the removal job down, and if called out again, you can charge them in line with the previous call-out. If called out, refer to the note book to see whether you have visited the site before.

Notes on migratory sites

Devote one single page per farm site. The notes should look something like this, as an example.

Leon and Jackie Broad phone, 023 555 3457

Children Mike and Sally, 12 and 15 years.

Leon works as a tire salesman in Kleindorp.

Leon and Jackie own the farm.

Inroad sketch.

<u>Wintering gum site</u>

Mixed gums flower July to March plus blackjack and cosmos from February to April.

Very muddy road into the site from the farm road to the homestead. Must phone during rainy weather if one goes into the site.

Dates last visited

12 03 2000 Moved onto site from Grootvlei sunflower. Bees generally strong a total of 34 hives each one super for cosmos.

15 04 2000 Visited Leon and gave 10 bottles of honey. Bees in good condition. Cosmos running out and can be robbed off on 30 April.

05 05 2000 Robbed off all hives taken down to broods only. Still plenty of blackjack flowering. Estimated 200 kilos of cosmos/blackjack honey.

10 08 2000 Spring cleaning done. Remove 6 dead hives now 28 on site each with one super.

31 08 2000 Visited Jackie and gave 8 bottles of honey. Now total of 18 bottles given.

14 09 2000 Additional super added. Took off 10 nucs for new queens.

22 09 2000   Inspected for queen cells. Six nucs have queen cells. United 4 nucs back to adult swarms where queens failed.

20 10 2000   Six nucs extended to brood boxes each with queen excluder and one super. Total hives on site 34.

10 12 2000   Visited the Broads' and gave 8 bottles of honey. Total now 26 for the year 2000. Robbed off 36 supers, approx. 320 kilos.

09 01 2001   Moved to Grootvlei sunflower 24 hives now 10 hive on site each with two supers.

Tales of an African Beekeeper

The tables on the following two pages are used to provide a record and summary of the hives per site, and the yield per site respectively:

Site Names	Date / Hives	Date / Hives	Date / Hives
	10 08 2000	12 10 2000	14 01 2001
Jackie Breedt	28	36	10
Dagga Mine	30	21	6
Rondebult substation	27	32	0

Table 1 : Hive Register

Site Names	Date / Kilo's	Date / Kilo's	Date / Kilo's
	10 08 2000	12 10 2000	14 01 2001
Jackie Breedt		200	
Dagga Mine		180	
Rondebult substation		260	

Table 2 : Honey Yield

"All the honey a bee gathers during its lifetime doesn't sweeten its sting."
Italian Proverb

24 Cropping and extracting honey

For the beginner hobbyist for his own table use

This method is for a beginner with one or two hives who draws one or two frames at a time, on average three bottles per frame.

Smoke the hive well at both entrances and any other leaky places through which bees are working, and leave for 30 seconds. Smoke again and leave for another 30 seconds. Prize the lid open with the hive tool and smoke well under the lid. Gently lift the lid and thump the bees off the lid in front of the hive with one stroke only. Smoke down between the frames to be removed, remove one, two or three capped frames from the centre of the super chamber, brush off the bees and hang the frames in an empty super chamber to be used as a carrying device. Move frames from the outside frames in the super to the centre of the super chamber and fill the spaces with new frames of full foundation or drawn comb. Replace the lid.

Time for the whole operation is 2 minutes.

The carbolic-cloth method

This is a method for beginners who wish to remove the entire honey-capped super. This method extends over a few days and is good when one is gaining confidence to work with bees.

Obtain a piece of thick blanket, or type of quilt cloth that can remain moist for a day or two. Soak this cloth in carbolic soap or oil solution and wring out so as not to be dripping wet but well moist, before use. Smoke at the entrances as before, but break the hive above the queen excluder and the bottom of the super leaving the lid intact and set aside on its end next to the hive. Place the new empty super over the queen excluder and replace the full super. Smoke at the entrances, and again lift the lid as before smoking under the lid. Place the carbolic cloth over the super frames and a sheet of plastic or newspaper onto the top of the carbolic cloth, and replace the lid. This newspaper or plastic is to prevent the carbolic odour from adhering to the underside of the lid which will deter the bees from re-entering the new super should there be this carbolic odour about. The bees immediately start vacating the super and the following evening the super can be removed with none or very few bees among the frames.

Time for the entire operation is 90 seconds.

A variation to this carbolic method is where one uses two cloths and all the frames are removed the same evening.

Have ready at hand two slightly moistened carbolic cloths as before and the super with the empty frames. A small table or stand is useful to rest the super onto while working. Smoke as before and remove the lid. Smoke the bees down between the honey-combs and place the one cloth over the frames. Leave for about 30 seconds. Now role the cloth from one end, smoke down and remove the first frame and then the second and third frames.

In the first frame position replace with an empty frame and draw the second cloth over the new frames as one proceeds across the super removing frame by frame. After the last frame has been removed remove the cloth and replace the lid, mission complete.

Time taken 2 minutes. Because of this long duration, one would need to constantly blow a puff or two across the entrance where the bees will come out to investigate the intruder.

This frame replacement method can be employed without using cloths but best with continual lightly smoking over the frames as one proceeds.

Utilizing a bee escape clearing board

The standard inner cover board that is standard equipment where telescopic lids are utilized, has an oval hole in the centre of the board. Purchase a small device that fits snugly into this hole known as a "one-way bee escape". This device has a sliding lid and inside are two small very soft springs. The springs are so positioned to allow the bees to pass down through the round hole on the top of the device and through the two springs. The springs open and close as each bee passes through but does not allow the bees to return into the super. One must constantly check these springs before the device is used to ensure that the bees have not propolised the springs together, which will prevent them from functioning properly.

Smoke the hive as previously mentioned, lift the super and lid together above the queen excluder. Place an empty super with drawn comb (preferably not all frames with foundation only) onto the queen excluder. On top of this empty super place the bee escape board and the full honey-super and bees and the attached lid. The super will be clear of bees after two days. If there are bees in the super, then the springs in the escape have been jammed by a drone bee and need to be cleared. This does sometimes happen and is the disadvantage of utilizing this method.

Cropping by using a basher box (for the more advanced hobbyist)

Have on hand the new super to replace the one to be removed, and a super chamber without frames, known as a "basher box". Place the basher box down on the ground in front of the hive.

Smoke as before, remove the lid and smoke down the bees between the frames. Remove the super above the queen excluder level and place on the basher box. Replace the new super and the lid. Gently thump the super onto the basher box about 8 times firmly in succession, but not to break the heavy framed honey-combs. The bees fall down on the ground. Remove the basher box about two meters away to the front of the hive. Investigate through the frames and brush off any adhering bees in the front of the hive. Duration time over the open hive should be about 30 seconds.

Most, most, most important!!!

It cannot be over-emphasized that whatever the method, *always* place the super that has received the honey frames into an empty carry super and onto a drip board and *cover immediately* with a good fitting lid. This is to prevent marauding bees that are flying about from setting up a robbing spree on any open and unprotected super containing honey-combs.

Where one is replacing supers with wet drawn comb supers, these too must be kept properly covered at all times to prevent a robbing spree from occurring. Should this robbing get under way, the entire cropping operation will turn into a fight of robbing bees and the operation will have to be abandoned until another time.

Extracting for the home hobbyist who utilizes one or two frames at a time

Work in a bee-proof room after dark (the kitchen sink is ideal, if permitted). Hold the frame vertically, scrape with a strong fork or comb all the honey and wax down to the foundation into a large sieve over a large mixing bowl. Mush up the mixture and allow it to stand for about two hours in a mild heated warming drawer. The honey and fine particles of wax will dribble down through the sieve. Tie a piece of moist muslin cloth over a second mixing bowl and pour the warm honey onto this muslin cloth stand in the warming drawer overnight. Switch off the warming drawer and by morning all the honey will have filtered through the cloth.

The course wax left in the sieve can be washed and dried out in the sun on a newspaper bed, or left away from the hives for the bees to clean. Should the honey guides find the wax (and make no mistake they do!), they will devour all the wax over a day or two. One frame will yield about 50 grams of wax, which can be collected and when say two hundred grams have been collected it can be melted in a double boiler and poured into a mould for other use.

Extracting machines

Other methods of extracting honey are by using machines known as honey frame extractors. The honey is uncapped using steam or electric uncapping knives and the frames placed vertically into special guides in the extractor cage and spun out by centrifugal force. Organizations selling these different machines will gladly demonstrate them.

"Veiled in this fragile filigree of wax is the essence of sunshine, golden and limpid, tasting of grassy meadows, mountain wildflowers, lavishly blooming orange trees, or scrubby desert weeds. Honey, even more than wine, is a reflection of place. If the process of grape to glass is alchemy, then the trail from blossom to bottle is one of reflection. The nectar collected by the bee is the spirit and sap of the plant, its sweetest juice. Honey is the flower transmuted, its scent and beauty transformed into aroma and taste."

Stephanie Rosenbaum

25 The ideal honey house

This description is for a medium sized honey house measuring 3.5m x 6m, approximately the size of a single garage, to accommodate an outfit of 1 to 300 hives and constructed as follows: Completely bee-proof room with ceilings, tiled and sealed floors, plastered washable painted walls and good lighting. Natural roof-light area over the extracting area is good. A wash hand basin with hot and cold water is required. Fan heaters are good for work during the winter days.

The honey house must be set up to extract honey, deal with wax cappings and other wax related operations, and to further bottle and store honey for future sales or bottling.

The extracting equipment should comprise a factory style production line system comprising:

A super frame lifting table

This comprises a small table with two parallel rails 30mm high securely screwed down onto the top, shorter than the inner dimensions of the width of the super chamber and fixed in such a position that when the super is placed over these two rails, the super frames are lifted above the rebate in the short sides of the super. In this way one can easily lift the frames without having to prize them out one by one, which will damage the frames.

An uncapping bin

A plastic 150 litre drum similar to the size and height of a municipal garbage bin complete with two handles is ideal. Tie netting around the top of the bin and hanging into the bin create a baggy net. Netting similar to plastic shade cloth is ideal. Across the top of the bin create a wooden cross frame that securely laps over the edges of the bin, this frame must fit securely. Onto this frame stand the honey frame to be uncapped. Cut the capping downwards so that the capping falls into the net and the clean honey will filter down through the net into the bin.

Drip trays. These are two trays size 460mm x 600mm x 250mm deep, the width and depth with a small clearance each side to hang a brood frame. If the extractor is a twenty-four frame unit, then these trays should hold 30 uncapped frames (15 each) ready for the next spin in the extractor.

The extractor

A twenty-four frame radial electrically driven extractor is sufficient for 300 hives. The extractor should stand on a frame with the outlet 600mm up from the floor so that a 25 litre drum can stand below the outlet. A large sieve is useful to hang into the drum to catch most of the cappings from the extractor. This extractor secured to its stand needs to be bolted down to the floor. One person, over a five hour working spell will extract 20 supers equal to 180 kilograms of honey.

Honey loaded supers are brought in from the apiary and stacked on the floor alongside the uncapping bin. A super is moved from the stacked supers to the small frame-lifting table. The frame is uncapped over the capping bin.

The extracted frames are placed back into the supers and stacked in another area until required for the next cropping occasion. The honey is allowed to settle out in the bottom of the extractor before tapping into drums or buckets. A great deal of wax flakes float to the top of the honey, which helps to clear the honey. At this stage the honey is suitable to be transferred to the bottling tank to be bottled as "raw honey." There should be an area to stack at least twelve twenty-litre drums.

A 100 litre hot water urn is useful. Inside and on the bottom of the urn place a metal frame stand to protect the element and the thermostat from being damaged by drums placed into the urn. Metal or plastic kegs or bottles or buckets, selected to suit the internal diameter of the urn. This urn is used to degranulate drums or buckets of granulated honey, to prepare the honey for bottling. Also used to melt wax cappings, clean honey for bottling, and generally to provide hot water whenever required.

After each extracting session of one or two days, clean the floor and generally clean up before setting up for the bottling operation. Do not mix extracting and bottling in the same work session.

Bottling department

A permanent metal top table is required and a 50 litre bottling drum with a small honey gate for filling honey bottles. A heated thermostatically controlled unit is ideal which will enable one to have honey on tap all the time. A storage area for about 30 boxes of empty bottles is required.

Good working practice is to record the cropped batch of supers. Say 32 supers from Reading golf club cropped 23/11/2007, bluegum honey, 540 bottles and the batch number written on the bottle. In this way any comebacks on the honey can be traced.

Bees in the honey house

Bees will collect in the honey house from the incoming supers and bees that have somehow flown in during the day in search of honey.

During the day do not let these bees out of the window. They will call other bees to the honey house. Leave them and deal with them at the end of the day at nightfall.

Hang a clean drawn comb brood frame at the top of the window. At nightfall all the bees in the honey house will settle on this frame. Then take the frame and shake it off or stand it near the entrance of a hive. By morning all the bees will have joined the hive.

Always lock the honey house – it is alarming how quickly a bottle of honey can disappear.

Always keep open drums of honey closed with loose lids. Should a rat fall into a drum of honey worth R900, what do you throw away – the rat or the honey?

Honey is a highly sought after food product and absolute cleanliness is the order of the day.

A Tale of a City Beekeeper

Pages of this book would be incomplete without a tale about a city beekeeper who resided in a double storey house in Kensington, an eastern suburb of Johannesburg. The home was built high on a rocky ledge with an outlook to the northern horizon where one would expect to find Pretoria. Above the upper storey was a large attic constructed within the roof structure that formed Kon's apiary site in which he kept up to thirty hives.

The hives were placed around the perimeter of the roof, each with its own entrance constructed in such a way as to appear slightly different from one another to prevent the bees from drifting, which happens if all the entrances are too similar. In the centre under a large warm roof light was the honey extractor cubicle, and slightly to one side the bottling area.

He had good access to each hive, usually fitted with two supers, and as Kon needed honey he would clear two or three supers utilising the one-way bee escape, extract the honey and return the supers back to the hives on a "same day" service system. In this way he reaped an average of one ton of honey annually, bottled and distributed to his local customers. All very compact and neat – no travelling to sites in windy, cold, or rainy weather, no stuck-in-the-mud situations, no vandalism, no staff – just Kon and his own two hands.

One under-estimated him as a city dweller, as he was an authority on trees, shrubs, indigenous flowers, large or small. He often hosted us to trips into the bushveld, especially at springtime, just to be away into the open country. He loved to point out the good nectar yielding plants and urged us not to just venture into the bushveld and hope for a good honey yield on a hit and miss system. But above all, the eucalyptus trees were his speciality. He could name them all – the good nectar yielders, the summer, winter, spring and autumn flowering varieties. He always frowned on anyone calling them just "blue gums."

Unfortunately Kon was very sensitive to bee venom and always had to take extra precautions when exposing himself to a possible bee sting and in spite of this hazard and for all the care he was conscious to take, one night at the early age of 65 years, he just slipped away in his sleep.

"The glob of precious honey that I had poured into my mouth at Ace's was the life's work of hundreds of bees, a unique floral ode collected from thousands of blossoms in a poetic foraging ritual..."

Holley Bishop

26 Wax processing and marketing

Firstly, the question, where does wax come from, how is it produced?

Bees need to consume honey in order to produce wax and therefore it is difficult for a starving swarm to be able to produce wax prolifically to build combs, but somehow they produce a small piece of comb. Once that is achieved, they are able to produce and store honey, and then to proceed to build more and more combs.

The comb comprises a multiple number of cells all built evenly to exact precision sizes and to the exact same depths, with the rows of combs at 32mm spacing centre to centre next to one another.

During the building process, there are two sets of bees performing two different functions. One set hangs in a curtain formation with legs joined one to the other – this defines the modular size of the cells. They are able, by working together, to construct small worker cells or larger drone size cells, depending on the size of cells required at the time. This set of bees secretes liquid wax from the six segments located on the undersides of their abdomens. As soon as this liquid wax comes into contact with the air, it solidifies into small flakes.

The second set of bees are the comb builders. They attach themselves to the curtain bees and remove the small flakes from the curtain bees' bodies and construct the midrib of the new comb. As this midrib progresses downwards the comb builders work side by side with the wax producers on both sides of the midrib to draw out the cells to their exact required depth. As the wax secretors become exhausted they rotate with other bees in order to maintain the supply of wax flakes for the comb builders until the comb has been completed.

It is remarkable to note that all this precision comb building is carried out in the pitch darkness of the hive!!! There are no consulting engineers, no architects or draughtsmen, no managers or supervisors, no onlookers no one getting into another's way, no tea or lunch breaks, no working to the clock – the work stops when the job has been completed. Surely mankind can learn something from this marvellous creation!

Sources of Wax

Wax is derived from the following sources:

1. Capping after extracting.

2. Combs from bee removal jobs that have been discarded.

3. Old super combs that have become black through constant use.

4. Clean-up of combs after wax moth invasion.

Wax Processing

The most valuable wax is from the cappings and damaged combs that have been cut out of bee removal undertakings (items 1 and 2 above). This selected light colored wax is not to be mixed with darker wax as that will bring down the value of the finished product. Also any wax that is mixed with honey has to have the honey removed, before the wax can be treated.

The recommended method is to mush up the cappings and allow the mixture to drain over a screen into drip trays of some design. Some beekeepers have special cages that fit into the extractor into which the cappings are tipped and spun out. The wax is then washed, allowed to dry, and then melted at 60°C in a double boiler and poured through a very fine sieve, such as nylon stockings, and into a suitable mould.

Absolute cleanliness is to receive priority. This is top class wax that one could sell to manufacturers of special creams used in cosmetics. The wax must be packed in very clean containers to satisfy the buyers of the absolute cleanliness practised throughout the wax collecting process. The asking price of this type of wax is approximately R180 per kilogram.

This wax can also be prepared for the beekeepers' wax trade. In this case, dump all the wet cappings and cut up comb into a metal keg. When the keg is full and weighs about 25kg, insert the keg into a double boiler, which is a hot water urn. Inside the urn at the bottom, have a wire metal reinforcing frame onto which the keg rests so as not to touch the heater element. It is a good idea to fit a fiberglass, insulated jacket around the urn to conserve heat and save electricity.

The thermostat is set for 70°C which melts the wax and slightly overheats the honey, which ideally should not be heated over 60°C. Monitor this process and after about four hours all the wax will be melted and floats on top of the honey. All impurities are suspended in the wax layer. Allow the entire contents to cool down. Remove the wax layer and all the suspended trash and you are left with clean honey. Reheat the honey to easy-pouring consistency, pour it through a muslin cloth strainer into the bottling tank. The resultant wax is usually a darkish amber color and is acceptable for rolling into foundation wax. This wax sells to the wax trade for around R40.00 per kilogram.

Wax extracted from items 3 and 4 is treated in another way.

One sorts out the black combs from any other textured colors. Cut out the black areas and discard or burn. There is absolutely no recoverable wax in these black combs. The honey must first be extracted as above utilizing the hot urn system. The other sections of the combs that do not have honey deposits are then placed in a solar heater and allowed to melt and drain away into metal trays or bread baking pans. This wax is fairly clean and varies in color from dark brown to dark cream and is rated as standard grade and sold for approximately R40 per kilo.

The solar heater is a most useful item in dealing with all types of dirty combs and frames and is a must in the beekeeper's kit. It is basically a hot box mounted at an angle of 30° to the sun, to utilize the sun's rays. It has a double glazed lid, a storage chamber and a space to receive one or two bread pans into which the wax drains away after passing through a sieve. The temperature inside the solar heater chamber rises to 90°C and above, which is too high for wax, causing it to darken and become rated as standard grade.

I collect these moulds of wax from the bread pans from the solar heater, place them into a metal keg and soak them in water to remove any honey. I then heat them to 70°C and pour off the wax through a metal screen into moulds until I notice the layer of dirt coming to the fore of the lip of the keg from which I am pouring. This last wax and dirt I pour into a separate flat tray for feeding through the solar wax heater again. The dirt remains suspended on screens placed onto the bottom of the solar heater and the wax separates into the bread pan of the solar heater.

Wax should not be heated above 80°C. Also propolis on the frames melts and mixes with the wax that causes darkening. Where one neglects to remove the melted wax in the solar heater and this wax is reheated, it will darken and if neglected over a week, the hot sunshine will turn the wax quite black rendering it useless even for the beekeeper wax foundation trade.

Unfortunately the honey from dark to black comb takes on a dark color and is rather unpleasant giving it an unacceptable sour taste and is best tipped out near an apiary for the bees to take. Often times they too refuse to take this honey.

Wax trading

Choice grade wax can be sold to the cosmetic market at R180 per kilogram.

Standard grade wax is traded for sheet foundation required by the beekeeper. There are 11 sheets of brood size foundation to the kilo and should one need to purchase 11 sheets of foundation, there will be an outlay of 11 x R10.00 = R110.00.

The beekeeper, before he sells standard grade wax, must top up his stocks of foundation wax for his own requirements. One way to do this is to exchange wax for foundation wax and pay just for the rolling – the going price for rolling is about R24.00 per kilogram.

In my case, I work in 13 kilogram lots which I box and send to Even-run Apiary Products in Pietermaritzburg. They roll the wax into brood size foundation sheets which they courier back to me. This transport costs R6.00 per kilogram per return trip. Total outlay for 13 kilograms for transport is R78.00.

The rolling of the wax costs R312.00 (13 kilos @ R24.00 per kilo), the transport costs R78.00 (13 kilos @ R6.00 per kilo), total equals R390.00 for 143 sheets (13 kilos @ 11 sheets per kilo). Therefore my brood size foundation sheet costs R2.73 per sheet.

As there is always a shortage of wax, especially in times of drought, it is best to trade all one's wax. Pay the rolling price and the courier transport costs and then you can sell the surplus sheets to fellow beekeepers. It is also good practice to keep the wax in the beekeepers' trade to prevent an eventual shortage of wax in the bee industry.

"The honey-bee that wanders all day long
The field, the woodland, and the garden o'er,
To gather in his fragrant winter store,
Humming in calm content his winter song,
Seeks not alone the rose's glowing breast,
The lily's dainty cup, the violet's lips,
But from all rank and noxious weeds he sips
The single drop of sweetness closely pressed
Within the poison chalice."
Anne Charlotte Lynch Botta

27 Pollination

God placed *Apis mellifera* (our variety is known as *scutellata*) on earth to pollinate the flowers, which produce the seed to replace the dying species of all plants – trees that provide shelter and bring the rain, grasses that provide grazing, weeds that provide compost, and nutritious fruits and vegetables in order to sustain man on earth. Albert Einstein, in a paper on bees, so correctly summed up the situation that should bees be eliminated from the earth, mankind would starve to death and would only be able to exist for five years.

Flowers are structured with stamens and a pistol and that sweet nectar that is secreted to lure the bee into the flower. Nectar and pollen are gathered in a balanced fashion. Should the swarm need pollen, the bees gather pollen only even from nectar yielding flowers. So a bee foraging for pollen, gathers pollen only and no nectar at the same time. Conversely, when nectar is required, the bees gather nectar only and overlook the pollen.

Therefore bees do not collect nectar and pollen on the same gathering flight trip.

Following on these facts, the pollination of cultivated crops is a most important function rendered by the beekeepers. In highly cultivated areas, natural pollinating insects hardly exist, as they have been exterminated by insecticides. Beekeepers are called into these areas to provide bees to perform the pollination. In cases where nectar is yielded by the flowers of the crop, the beekeeper gets his honey, which is regarded as sufficient reward for his efforts. On these occasions the beekeeper who seeks honey for his living asks for sites and is usually most welcome. These crops are commercial sunflower growers, citrus, litchis and kidney bean crops.

However, where no honey is obtained and the swarms become weaker, the beekeeper charges for the pollination service. These crops are pumpkins, cherries, kiwi fruits, apples, pears, all deciduous fruits, berry fruits and most varieties of nuts. The biggest pollination contracts are for sunflower seed production, for seed required by the commercial sunflower growers and the fruit industry especially in the Western Cape.

Beekeepers should be encouraged to progress beyond honey production and extend into pollination of cultivated crops. As our fruit industry increases, so too should the bee pollination industry increase. The areas around Ermelo are becoming a great apple growing area in South Africa and the bee industry would be lacking if it did not seize the opportunities that lie ahead to pollinate the apples of these areas. This applies as well to cherries and apples grown in the Eastern Free State around Ficksburg and Bethlehem.

*"The pedigree of honey
Does not concern the bee;
A clover, any time, to him
Is aristocracy."*
Emily Dickinson

28 Granulation

"What causes granulation?" is the question often posed. Because of the manipulation of so many products and so many manufactured goods, the poor housewife, who is out to find the best for her family in pure good food, suspects that the beekeeper is also up to his tricks. She concludes that because the honey granulates, it has "gone off", and so she dumps it in the refuse bin. When dark honey granulates it does look damn terrible and one does not blame her. So she becomes very wary of honey and refrains from further purchasing the product.

Let's get down to the truth of the matter. No matter what the beekeeper says about the various natural sugars reacting with one another, he is at the root of all evil and the granulation process. Take for example a hive with two supers full of honey and only one super is removed and extracted. Within three weeks after extracting the honey granulates. After a further month the beekeeper removes the second super and there is no granulation in the comb honey.

So what has happened?

Firstly, let's go back in time a little to the last robbing of the previous season, about last May. The honey-wet supers were stacked in the closed shed and possibly covered to prevent wax moth and mice invasion. Had they been put outside for the bees before storing away, the bees would have licked them clean, but small deposits, or a film of honey was left on the walls of the cells which has granulated, and formed a perfect seeding for the new honey. The answer is to wash the supers before they are reused again.

Secondly, the beekeeper robs off in the late afternoon or at night. He stacks the open uncovered supers on the open lorry or trailer and with hard pumped up tires and a cool breeze, over a corrugated road he sets off to the honey house. This type of treatment rapidly induces granulation. Therefore he should have worked in the warmth of the day, used a closed vehicle, closed down the supers, slightly deflated the tyres and carefully picked his way to make the best of the corrugated road back to the honey house.

Thirdly, into the cool honey house he stacks his supers and for rapid completion of the entire operation he tends to thump and bump his supers while off-loading. More granulation inducement, because the supers should be gently off-loaded and placed into a warm cupboard or small heated chamber (at a temperature of about 35°C).

Fourthly, he is only able to extract the supers after two or three days and in the coolness of the environment he incurs more granulation problems. Ideally he should start extracting that same day of cropping or at the latest the very next day. Therefore he should plan his cropping on the day when he is able to extract the honey.

Tales of an African Beekeeper

Problem number five is the condition of the extractor. From the previous operation there will most definitely be a thin film of granulated honey on the walls of the extractor, which will create a perfect seeding for the new honey. So keep the extractor as clean as possible.

A cool honey house and an open radial extractor that draws the cool air into the extractor as the fine threaded honey spins to the sides of the extractor spells more trouble, so the honey house ideally should be warmed (35°C) and the extractor closed when in operation.

Then this thin, flowing, cooled, vibrated and aerated honey is often stored in a plastic or metal keg that too has a fine film of granulated honey down the inside walls. What chance does the beekeeper give himself?

Finally, the honey is heated for bottling and labeled as "pure unadulterated honey". If overheated, the honey will turn darker than is necessary. The housewife buys this darkened honey and after a month on the shopkeeper's shelves and three weeks in the housewife's cupboard it starts to granulate and appears as a sugary dark gunk which she dumps vowing never to buy honey again. The trick here is not to allow the honey to stand too long on the supermarket shelves. Rather encourage the shop to take smaller orders more frequently so that the honey shifts rather than stands. Offer a customer exchange service to shopkeepers, and do not allow them to degranulate the honey – they can really mess up the honey and the label.

Rather do the bee industry a good service by educating the housewife to the effect that only pure honey will granulate. Perhaps a small compact label added to the bottle explaining the fact that granulation is caused by the natural sugars of honey reacting with one another and a brief description of how to degranulate the honey by the heating process.

Different types of honey have different granulation duration periods. Sunflower, cosmos and aloe honey, which are quick crops, granulate quicker that eucalyptus and multiflora that are long duration crops to be gathered in by the bees. All depends on the proportions of the various natural sugars that combined together to form honey. Only pure honey will granulate, and granulation is a natural process of honey, whether extracted or stored in the combs that preserves honey over very long periods. Simply by heating honey the granulation breaks down and the honey is reduced to its liquid form again which is easier for human consumption. There are no natural steps that one can take to prevent granulation, so at best, we want to retard or slow the granulation process.

Tips to retard the granulation process

Never stack wet supers away in a store. After extracting the honey, the supers can be stacked three or four high onto a hive. The bees will clean out all the honey and remove it down to their own super or brood chamber. Them remove the supers and store them under cover.

A good method is to place two timber slats onto a metal tray on the floor, onto which place a queen excluder or a fine mesh screen and then stack the supers ten or twelve high. Place a queen excluder or fine wire mesh on top of the top super and brick thereon to prevent mice from entering the super stack – they can cause irreparable damage. This method of screens allows a draught to pass through the supers. Many wax flakes fall to the metal tray which can be collected and melted for reuse.

After extracting, clean the extractor and other utensils used during the extracting process, this prepares for the next time, and with beekeepers there is always a next time.

Crop the honey super during the warmth of the day, brush the bees off the honey combs rather that thump them off with a shaker.

Deflate the vehicle or trailer tires especially if one is riding over corrugated roads and drive moderately slowly.

Before setting out switch the heaters on in the honey house to warm the room to approximately 35ºC.

Avoid thumping the supers when loading from the hives and off-loading from the vehicle and stack them criss-cross in an open fashion in the honey house or extracting room to allow the warm air to percolate through the supers. An electric blanket wrapped around the supers is a good method to warm the supers instead of preheating the honey house.

Proceed with the extracting as soon as possible after entering the honey house.

An electric blanket wrapped around the extractor is also a good method to warm the extracting procedure. However the best method is to heat the entire honey house if possible.

Keep the extractor lid closed while the extracting is in progress to avoid cool air being drawn into the extractor.

The drum or bucket to receive the extracted honey from the extractor should be clean and free from any previous honey remains that may have started granulating.

When bottling the honey, warm the bottles first and bottle the honey at 60°C.

"The careful insect 'midst his works I view,
Now from the flowers exhaust the fragrant dew,
With golden treasures load his little thighs,
And steer his distant journey through the skies."
John Gay

29 Occupational hazards

Beekeeping, like any other farming occupation, has its occupational hazards, some folk survive and others fail. There is a Scottish saying, "It's the master's eye that fattens the ox". And so too it's the beekeeper, unafraid to get stuck in himself with smoker and hive tool, that leads the way among his workers – as with the bees themselves, there are no 'passengers'.

These are some of the hazards that can be overcome by the beekeeper:

Vandalism

We throw up our arms and say vandalism is killing the industry. So build good secure bee camps, provide 'booby traps' in the camps, and the word quickly gets around that these camps are no-go areas.

Fires

Keep the camps and 2m wide surrounds to the camps clear of grass and weeds that will burn. Better still, pave the camps and the surrounds and the annual job of spraying expensive weed killer and cleaning up is eliminated.

Annual 20% swarm replacement

Have a regular annual swarm replacement program in place, whether it be catching feral swarms or a queen breeding program to replace exhausted queens.

Migrant worker syndrome

Beekeeping is hard work, often into the night and early hours of the morning. A trained worker is an irreplaceable commodity and must be nurtured. Provide decent accommodation for him, pay him well and reward him generously as the pocket will allow.

Vehicles

Nothing worse than a breakdown with a load of bees on board! Keep the tires in good condition to minimize punctures. Service vehicles regularly and replace on a regular basis to avoid riding around in an oldish rattletrap.

Site owner relationships

Good tested sites are most valuable. Therefore it is most important to conduct oneself in a most responsible manner when entering these sites. This must be stressed upon the workers, especially when entering farms at night or in the early hours of the morning before daybreak. Always remember that you as a beekeeper do not own the land. You have merely been given the right of way onto farm land or any other land for that matter. Keep in regular touch with the landowner with a visit. Some honey always pays good dividends. To loose a good site due to bad behavior is an unforgivable error.

Tales of an African Beekeeper

Shared sites

The landowner can allow as many beekeepers onto his land as pleases him. In a diplomatic way one has to overcome this hazard. One way is to impress upon the landowner the risk that the other beekeeper could remove one's hives "quite innocently and in error". If this situation cannot be resolved with the landowner and the other beekeeper it is best to abandon the site altogether. Niggardly arguments merely waste valuable beekeeping time.

Loss of bees due to crop spraying

In areas where spraying is essential one has to comply with the farmer's program, by closing down the bees for the duration of the spraying or removing the hives during the spraying period. Spraying by airplane can kill an entire apiary in one day. Impress upon the farmer the severity of this hazard and if he fails to cooperate, blacklist him via your association for any future pollination services.

There are some hazards that the beekeeper is *unable* to control:

Diseases among bees

It is a peculiar phenomenon when an unexpected disease suddenly raises its head – as we experienced with "black bee pseudo queen syndrome", or as we all named it "Capensis invasion". Who knows if next we suddenly have American Foul Brood disease? In cases like these, we can only turn to research and the universities to investigate these problems.

Peter L Clark

Importation of Honey

The Department of Trade and Industry (DTI) grants the permits for importation of cheap honey and the beekeeper throws up his arms in despair. At the cost of minimum wages dictated to him and the unstable fuel price he cannot compete with the price of imported honey. However a bottler who has never seen the inside of a beehive can cut him down and put him completely out of business.

The Department of Agriculture is crying out for beekeepers to pollinate the crops, and the DTI is simultaneously putting them out of business. There is no consultation with other role players in the industry affected by the import permit, the permit is simply granted.

Eradication of eucalyptus trees

The Department of Agriculture are saying we need a further 20,000 beekeepers to meet future requirements. The Department of Water Affairs ("working for water") is saying, "remove all the alien gum trees", and the beekeeper, that needs these trees to carry his bees until the next pollination season, throws up his arms in despair again. This practice is ongoing despite our plea to the Department of Water Affairs.

The high cost of fuel

How does one keep accurate costs of operations of migratory pollination services and specialized honey production where there are continuing fluctuations in the fuel price? Surely, if properly managed, there are government subsidies that could be applied, as these services are so vital to the farming industry.

Tales of an African Beekeeper

It is these hazards, beyond the control of the beekeeper and beyond his reach as an individual, that create the demand for a strong body representing the beekeepers and their various Associations to combat these hazards on their behalf. The South African Beekeepers Industry Organisation (SABIO) was established some years ago to achieve this.

In Australia, New Zealand and America beekeepers are highly regarded important role players in the farming industry thanks to interaction with, and lobbying of, various levels of government.

A final warning about "Apiculturitis" – the disease your will get when keeping bees for a lengthy period of time. The travelling about the country, meeting farmers, the fresh air, and the feeling that you are the last of the free, getting drenched in the rain and stuck in the mud grows on you as an incurable disease........love the life !!

<u>Notes</u>

"The men of experiment are like the ant, they only collect and use; the reasoners resemble spiders, who make cobwebs out of their own substance. But the bee takes the middle course, it gathers its material from the flowers of the garden and field, but transforms and digests it by a power of its own."

~ *Francis Bacon*

30 The problem of pseudo queens

(also known as black bee, or capensis invaders)

If you are experiencing any of the following problems, then this chapter will be of particular interest to you:

- Swarms dying out for no reason;

- Unable to rear new queens;

- Swarms absconding.

During the late 1980s a certain beekeeper from the Cape migrated Apis capensis bees to Bushbuckridge in the heart of an Apis scutellata area. These are two totally different strains of bees and the mixing of these strains created an interbreeding of the two species which had a devastating effect on the scutellata bees.

A strange bee evolved, very similar in total appearance and size to a scutellata worker. This bee carries a queen pheromone and the scutellata bees accept it as a scutellata queen. This bee does not lay eggs that produce worker bees, but lays eggs that produce its own strain. It does not forage but only exists on the stores of the swarm, and they do not sting as readily as scutellata workers.

These bees have become so widespread in the scutellata areas that each and every swarm is suspected to be carrying them. They exist in small numbers, maybe only twenty in a hive. Because they do not forage, they are long living, possibly longer than a year and because they carry a queen pheromone, the bees simply accept them. However, they fear the queen and live above the queen excluder and for this reason beekeepers are operating without queen excluders so that they are able to expose these bees to the queen who hopefully will kill them as she is much larger and stronger than them. So, as long as the queen is present, they remain dormant, but there comes a time when the queen is not present and it is at this period that these bees raise their ugly heads.

It is natural for bees to swarm off and the queen leaves the swarm to set up home elsewhere and the swarm is left to develop a new queen. During this queenless period these pseudo queens develop into a laying mode. Now their appearance changes to shiny black bees who struggle to squeeze through the queen excluder and for the first time they are easily detected by the beekeeper. They lay their eggs, as many as ten to twelve in one cell, often in the larger drone cells. The nurse bees remove these eggs and place them one by one individually into a vacant cell. Hence one finds this scattered brood that is one of the indications of the presence of these foreign bees. Because of the presence of this queen pheromone of these pseudo queens, the bees do not attempt to raise a new replacement queen and the swarm exists queenless with no further replacements of lost worker bees. Eventually the food stores are totally consumed, the scutellata worker bees starve to death and the pseudo queens move into the adjacent hives in the apiary. Because of the queen pheromone odour they carry, the guard bees of the adjoining hives allow them into the hives but not the foreign starving scutellata workers.

Of course, by this stage they have increased immensely in numbers and move into virtually all the other thirty hives in the apiary, causing the entire apiary to eventually die out.

The beekeeper's attempt to raise new queens fails because he has to remove the queen from the swarm to induce the bees to build and raise queen cells and the presence of the pseudo queens prevents the bees from doing so.

The only solution to the problem is to kill the entire swarm once these pseudo queens are detected and to examine the adjoining swarms which may also need to be destroyed before the entire apiary is lost.

<u>Notes</u>

"...the rules of the LORD are true, and righteous altogether. More to be desired are they than gold, even much fine gold; sweeter also than honey and drippings of the honeycomb."
Psalm 19:9 – 10, ESV

31 Tips to enjoy your beekeeping

One must enjoy beekeeping, and to achieve this, one needs the inward confidence to open a hive and work with the bees or to remove bees.

This confidence is acquired over a period of time and comes with frequent working with bees. One's subconscious mind must not be pre-occupied by circumstances brought about by the beekeeper himself, who is at the root of the entire dilemma. Being fearful, or having uncontrolled nerves, sets up undetected vibrations on the surface of one's skin and the surface skin hairs. These vibrations are detected by the bees ,which in turn causes them to become aroused and short-tempered.

If the following elements are correct and therefore not on the mind of the beekeeper, that inner fear of things going wrong will not harass the beekeeper before he starts.

The Beekeeper

The beekeeper needs:

1) Good, reliable, working and fitting veil, gloves and boots to enable him to move about freely and with

agile movements. At all costs avoid woollen or leather outer garments. Leather gloves are unacceptable.

2) Good, reliable smoker and correct fuel to suit the smoker.

3) Always plan ahead and know exactly what one is expecting to do and have the necessary equipment at hand to perform the operation.

4) Consult with another beekeeper about the operation to be undertaken, perhaps for advice or a helping hand.

5) Work clean so as not to leave comb lying about the apiary after one has completed the mission.

The apiary site

The site needs to be in a good secure area away from the paths of vandals and not too far from home base.

If possible stand the bees in partial shade especially protected against the afternoon sun in summer, and also in sheltered areas away from the cold south winter winds.

Place hives away from smelly, smoldering compost heaps, animal camps, poultry runs, and especially horse stables and smelly dog kennels.

Be aware of storm water flooding during heavy rainy weather and swampy areas that would deter the beekeeper from entering the site.

Wherever possible construct bee camps as an added protection against wandering animals that could disturb or overturn hives.

Keep grass and weeds away from the flight path of the worker bees. Wispy strands of grass waving in the wind that continually knock incoming workers down, create short-tempered workers.

Working time

Always work into the night. The best time to start is half an hour before sunset and then work half an hour into the night. As darkness sets in, one's vision becomes accustomed to the reducing daylight. Avoid using a light whenever possible as this tends to blind one and reflections on the veil material become distracting.

Open hives for a minimum of time. Two minutes at one spell is regarded as a long time.

Good relations

A bottle of honey for the owner of the plot or the farm always spreads goodwill wherever it sticks and touches.

Finally, some sage advice from Rudyard Kipling (with an apology for the minor modification),

> "If you can keep your head when all about you are loosing theirs, and blaming it on you, you'll be a good beekeeper, my son."

<u>Notes</u>

"The solitary Bee
Whose buzzing was the only sound of life,
Flew there on restless wing,
Seeking in vain one blossom where to fix."
Robert Southey

32 Conclusion

Many countries have lost their bee population and have to resort to hand pollination of fruit and vegetable crops. These losses have been due to careless spraying of insecticides, careless migratory handling of bee colonies, stressing bees and extreme damp and cold weather over long periods to mention only a few factors.

The departments of agriculture and leading entomologists of those countries are looking to South Africa to help formulate a plan to reestablish their bee populations by utilizing our bees. Our African bees are rated as the strongest race of bees in the world.

Let this serious situation serve as a warning to us that we too could loose our bees through careless handling. Pollution of water and the air and the irresponsible spraying of crops that enters the minute systems of the flying bee in all weather and dusty conditions already puts our bees at risk.

Therefore the appeal goes out to all – beekeepers, farmers, city dwellers, and industry – have mercy on our bees, love them and take good care of them. Should the world loose its entire bee population, the pollination of the food crops would fail, and to echo Albert Einstein's concluding research into the value of bees, "without bees, mankind will not survive longer than three to five years."

In my final paragraph allow me to iterate that I have enjoyed sharing my knowledge and experience, and urge all beekeepers to keep up the good work. Within the next twenty years the present beekeeping fraternity will need replacement and it is up to us to train interested newcomers and make sure that the "bee bug bites them". They will be required to continue to foster and manage bees to provide for the pollination of crops so vital to our very existence.

"The sweetest honey
Is loathsome in his own deliciousness
And in the taste confounds the appetite."
William Shakespeare

33 Appendix A: General Management Pointers

Work planning

- Set targets for the calendar year.

- Targets are based on previously-kept good and meaningful records.

- Migrants must plan their routes and sequence of sites.

- Set out catching programs to replace lost swarms as this is an ongoing task throughout the year.

Equipment

- Keep your equipment in good order, especially your vehicle which must be reliable at all times.

- Keep veils, gloves, clothing, smoker, night-light, honey-house equipment and all the hives always in good order.

- Clean out all redundant and dead hives and wax-moth and set out to catch new swarms.

Your bees

- Love your bees with unconditional love, always forgiving the odd sting.

- No passenger are allowed.

- Keep checking for black bee pseudo queen invasion and kill.

- Should you come across anything strange and suspect a disease, report this to your association.

Yourself

- Keep healthy. As far as possible, avoid climbing onto roofs and up ladders and take care of your limbs because to fall and break an arm or leg spells disaster.

- Join a beekeepers' association and mix around with beekeepers to keep abreast with what is going on all the time.

- Should you come across another beekeeper at a flea market or any other meeting place, chat him up, you and he are on common ground.

Your sites

- Good sites are the secret of the success of your beekeeping.

- Honey yields on good sites must not be disclosed to anyone.

- Avoid discussing sites.

- Always be on the look-out for better sites as they do exist and need to be found.

Good relations

Keep good relations:

- with your staff, after all trained staff are irreplaceable.

- with your farmer , who allows you onto his land, and drink coffee with his wife.

- with folk who are over authority over you, such as municipal inspectors etc.

Tales of an African Beekeeper

Your honey market

Service your customers diligently. Rather have few markets well-supplied, than many markets poorly-supplied. You will lose a poorly serviced customer to another beekeeper for ever.

Your fellow beekeepers

Share your knowledge and experiences with your fellow beekeeper but not your secrets. He will also share his, but not his secrets. Avoid picking his brain – that will shy him off completely.

<u>Notes</u>

34 Appendix B: Seasonal Management

This section is specific to the Gauteng area of South Africa. In this area, the year is broken down into the four seasons as follows:

Spring   July to October

Summer   October to March

Autumn   April and May

Winter   June to mid-July

Gauteng experiences summer rainfall, with an annual rainfall of 800mm. The summer temperatures range from 12ºC to 30 ºC. There is minimal rainfall in winter, but temperatures fall right down to -4ºC to 12 ºC, with frost.

34.1 Summer management

The summer season will yield two crops of honey in the Gauteng area, namely, the gum flow in October and November, a dearth period in December, a gum flow in January and cosmos and blackjack in February and March.

The important and tricky manoeuvre is when to super-up, when to crop the honey, and when to start closing down for the winter.

To understand the significance of summer management, one first needs to know briefly about spring cleaning.

Spring cleaning is performed as an annual beehive manoeuvre during the period from mid-August to end of

September when the hives are prepared for the summer honey flow. Briefly two old combs, usually the two outer combs in the brood chamber, are removed and replaced with two new frames of sheet foundation wax, or two good quality drawn combs which had been produced the previous season by bees from another swarm, and placed in the centre of the brood chamber.

After the spring cleaning in August, the hives will have built up considerably by October with a good population of young worker bees. This too, is the time when more honey storage space will be required and one of the secrets of success is how to give this space without discouraging the bees.

The new beekeeper has no option but to place a new super, preferably with nine frames and not ten frames, with wax foundation sheets onto the brood chamber. A queen excluder should be placed between the super and the top of the brood. Unfortunately a super with wax foundation only, presents a lot of work for the bees, and because of the cold spells and rather cool nights, the bees will not venture into the supers until well into the gum flow period and about 60% of the first honey crop will be lost. A super with strips of foundation only is even worse and does not encourage bees to work above the queen excluder at all. Where there is no proper guidance in strip foundation or full foundation in the frames, the bees will cross-build the honey combs in the super in any haphazard arrangement which later produces one terrible headache when removing the honey.

In the situation where a half-filled super is on the hive at the beginning of October, the presence of this new worker force generates more bodily heat in the brood chamber, which induces swarming, and for this reason, October is the principal swarming period.

The next secret of success is to prevent the bees from swarming off where one would lose 60% of this worker force. An additional super, preferably with drawn but empty combs, must be placed on top of the half-filled super to create this additional space in the hive to discourage this swarming. If this is to be provided timorously it is best done by mid-September. If one is forced to provide a foundation-only super, keep the queen excluder out until the bees are working in the super. Once the super is occupied and comb building is in progress, smoke the bees down, drum on the sides of the super to make sure that the queen has gone down, and then the excluder can be put into place above the brood chamber.

At the end of October, if one has a completely capped drawn comb super, place the new empty super below this super and on top of the queen excluder. After about two weeks the bees will have been placing honey in this second super and the top super can be removed. By the end of November this second super should be filled and capped.

However, do not remove all the early summer honey in November as the bees will most likely abscond and leave one with an empty hive.

December presents a dearth period and there is a shortage of nectar and pollen and the hives are best left alone with that full super until about the third week of January when the cosmos and black-jack flow commences. At this time, place an empty super below this full super. When the bees are working in this empty super, remove the full super. This is the second filled super from the hive and can be removed at the beginning of March. There is still enough forage remaining until the end of April for the bees to gather their winter stocks into the last remaining super, in which six full but uncapped frames will be sufficient.

By removing honey and still leaving honey on the hive, the risk of the bees absconding is greatly reduced. Should one remove that filled super before or during this dearth period, the bees are sure to abscond.

As the cold nights set in for the winter, the bees will be moving honey down to vacant cells in the brood chamber.

Another method to remove honey is to retain only one super on the hives throughout the summer and continually visit the hives throughout the summer season, say once a month, and remove only the capped frames. These frames will be found in the middle of the super, then move the outer frames to the centre and add the new empty frames to the sides, and at the end of March, leave six frames for the winter.

34.2 Winter management

This is an important time of organized beekeeping because it sets the swarm on a strong footing for the new season if properly handled. Bees and the beekeeper need a rest period and without a rest working life becomes an unwilling slog. This is found very strongly in the bee society. The queen must rest for approximately 10 weeks from end of April to mid-July.

In tropical and sub-tropical areas where no frosts occur there are marked times of flowering of certain flora and crops and it is between these times that the bees rest.

So, from the end of April to the end of June the beekeeper and the bees should take life a little slower.

What's happening in the floral kingdom?

As the nights lengthen and become colder, flowers become less. The cold shuts off any honey flow, especially the black iron bark. One will notice an abundance of flower buds on the Rhus Lanceas and, by the fullness of these buds, one can judge more or less as to the expectance of the early spring. Throughout the countryside, aloe arboresens will be flowering but does not yield much nectar. Eucalyptus robusta will be flowering and yields good nectar and pollen but not many trees occur to yield a honey flow.

What's happening in the beehive?

The queen reacts to this shortage of food and accordingly reduces the extent of her laying period as well as the amount of eggs laid daily and so the brood nest reduces to a small patch but does not disappear completely. Bees move honey from the outer combs and pack into these empty cells as an insulation in order to assist in keeping the brood warm.

The role of the beekeeper

Remove the metal queen excluders and all the supers that draw the cold into the hive.

Close down the lid tightly and plug up large holes around the hive parts. The bees will seal up the small cracks. At this point let's stress the importance of good lids and floors.

Place the hives in sheltered areas facing east to north, away from penetration of the south wind.

Small narrow nucs or modern plastic catch boxes should have extra wrapping and protection from cold penetration.

What's happening in the honey house?

This is cleanup time.

Put out for the bees all those wet supers, some of which will have granulation in the walls of the cells. Stack the supers criss-cross taking precautions to prevent mice from entering and damaging the drawn combs – they can cause absolute havoc. Pour about ten litres of water over the stack of supers to assist the bees to clean out the granulated honey. Collect the capping of wax that the bees dislodge and place them in the solar heater. Render and melt down all wax cappings etc. and send off to the wax processors in exchange for foundation wax which one will be needing in the early spring for the spring cleaning.

Tales of an African Beekeeper

Jobs around the bee camps

This is the time for site jobs. Clean up and cut the grass in order to prevent fires around your hives. Vandals will have been at your camps so you need to repair where damaged, and improve where they had gained access to prevent re-entry next year. It is also perhaps time to build a new bee camp or two as you expand your business.

Jobs in the workshop

Here the work is endless and not a moment should be spared asking, "what can be done?" There is all the cleaning of queen excluders and general maintenance of the equipment and the chance to knock a few more hives together for the next season. Perhaps the honey extractor needs attention. The bee veils can do with a clean and inspection to repair holes and tears, and of course don't forget to service the smoker. This is also a good time to service the vehicle, and maybe even replace a tire or two.

Feeding the bees

The bees can be fed pollen substitute during the winter months. There are various formulas listed in the "blue book" of beekeeping in South Africa. The cheapest is plain ground white mielie meal – best if one can obtain it freshly milled from a dairy farmer. Simply place the mielie meal in a shallow plastic lid on top of the brood frames under the lid. This winter feed, if accepted by the bees, will definitely give them a good kick start in the early Spring. See to it that enough honey was left behind in the hive for winter. If not, then feed equal quantities of white sugar and water inside the hive.

34.3 Spring management

Early Spring is the beginning of August in the southern hemisphere, but in colder areas, Spring starts a month later, at the beginning of September.

The sun is warming, the shortest day has passed by, the days are lengthening, and the Rhus Lancias and Acacia baileyanas are flowering. In the bushveld the Aloe Davyanas are the first pollen providers before the other flowering trees and plants. Mother Nature has provided pollen secreting plants first as it is pollen that the bees require to start brood rearing and the worker bees start pouring into the hive with pollen sacks on their back legs, loaded heavy with pollen granules.

With the warmer weather, the black iron bark, Eucalyptus Sideroxilyn will be secreting nectar again until about the end of August. Make no mistake, the bees are very sensitive to these changes and the beekeeper, before he knows it, is rustled back into action for the next season. He should have taken his leave and rest when the bees rested because from now on it is go, go, go.

Spring cleaning

The reason for spring cleaning is to provide space for the new developing brood at the outset of the new season.

At the start of the winter, around the end of March as the temperatures fall below 14°C, the bees slow down brood rearing. As the empty cells in the brood chamber are not reused, the bees pack honey in these cells. This brood area becomes smaller and smaller and the honey is packed down to create insulation for the minor brood development during the winter months. Honey is also removed from the super and drawn down into the brood chamber. Therefore it is imperative to leave sufficient honey for the swarm over the winter, but in the spring this honey is a problem for the new season's brood rearing. Because the bees are confined in a brood box there is no space for the expansion of the brood which would be the case if the swarm was located in a natural vast area such as in a roof or large box.

At the end of August it's into the brood chambers we must go. Sort through the frames and remove the two worst frames. The grading of the worst frames is as follows, in the order of worst frames first:

1) Drone brood combs where drone brood occurs in more than 10% of the frame.

2) Old black combs where worker cells are getting smaller, due to frequent usage during the previous seasons.

3) Badly or partly cross-built combs and poorly developed combs.

4) Honey frames where one would consider there is too much honey for the bees to move in order to create more laying space for the developing queen.

Having removed the two worst frames, move the remaining frames to the outer areas of the brood chamber, but keep the small brood area that does exist intact in the centre of the brood chamber. Place two frames of full sheet foundation, one on each side of the brood area into the brood nest so as not to divide the brood nest.

The term "Spring management" is also used where brood rearing space is to be provided during the summer months. Now suppose the bees have been on the gums from August to January and one intends to move them to sunflower at, say, Settlers from January to April, or to the Saligna in the Lowveld January to May.

Unless space is created in the brood rearing area, they will swarm off. To avoid this swarming, "spring cleaning" has to be employed and usually on these occasions one would need to remove two capped brood frames of solid honey on either side of the brood nest, and replace with two brood frames with full sheets of foundation within the brood nest area. This is done by placing these frames of foundation between brood developing frames. One can also provide this extra space by providing an extra super above the queen excluder, especially during hot summer sunny days to relieve heat build up in the hive.

This manoeuvre creates a large area in the brood nest for the early rearing of many more workers and more worker bees means better performance and more honey.

To the beekeeper who has not practiced spring cleaning before, give it a go next early spring season and marvel at the great improvement to the production of your swarms.

35 Appendix C: Floral Calendar

Gauteng Highveld

Different climatic areas have different flora e.g. north of the Magaliesberg is totally different to the Witwatersrand and so too is Ermelo and Vereeniging quite different from these places. Therefore, if one resides in Sandton and keeps bees in Ermelo, one needs to know the flora cycle of that area, and seasonal planning must relate to that area.

For most beekeepers our year starts on the 21 June, the shortest day, and therefore for simple understanding of the sequence of the flora, I am going to progress through the seasons of the year. During this time the bees are at their lowest ebb and are regarded as dormant. A few will be flying because of a warm day always on the lookout for a morsel and will be bringing in water and will always be on the search for a free coke down at the sports stadium.

The first food, required for the new developing brood cycles of the brood of the new season is protein. Therefore Mother Nature provides the first plants which are pollen yielding plants. In early July these are the Rhus Lancias and the Bailyanas. Then comes the early soft fruits in August and September viz the peaches, apricots, plums, cherries and a host of berry type fruits, both exotic and indigenous. October, by now the queens are in full laying cycles, the nectar yielding trees as the oaks, the eucalyptus Melliodora, the bottle-brush and a host of exotic flowering shrubs and general garden flowers are flowering. Heavily loaded bees continue to pour nectar and pollen into the hives as though a great famine is lurking at our doorsteps. One can walk around the apiary and among the hives without interference. November sees the toning off of this early summer flowering period and the setting of fruits that will later shed seeds.

December is the great dearth month. The main flowering period is over and it is the main fruiting month. There are very few flowers about, and the bees are ratty and impatient so back to the stadium for a free coke or two. To walk through the apiary and among the hives would be looking for inquisitive bees and trouble during this period.

Still on the highveld, the summer crops to flower in January to end of April are Eucalyptus, of many varieties, the main type being Eucl. Camaldulensis (Red river gum). Wild statice, khaki-bos, and cosmos and the main cultivated crops are sunflower and kidney beans.

Eucalyptus Sideroxylon (black iron bark) is our bonus gum and flowers from March through the winter to end of July. It is a nectar-yielding tree and ceases to yield once the cold weather starts. Bees only gather nectar from these trees when there is pollen about from whatever other sources.

Mpumulanga Lowveld

Now let us consider another area such as the Lowveld, down the Elands valley from Waterval Onder to Nelspruit where there is a host of different nectar yielding plants. The season in this area starts in July and into August with the flowering of many varieties of aloes. Then follows citrus, litchis, and many minor soft fruits and berries in September to November. December and January yields Avocados, Macadamia nuts, and the season concludes with Eucalyptus Saligna that flowers in

February to May. June is the rest month. Depending where the apiary is located most of these crops can be gathered from one site, not having to migrate the bees.

Thus different parts of the country can all be analyzed according to its own particular crops of flora. The Cape, for example, is quite different again and rather unique in the world because of the great variety of flora.

A hobbyist beekeeper with 10 to 20 hives can also have a lot of fun and reward by seeking a specific type of honey such as rosemary, chili, pumpkin or lavender honey. He first scouts around to find a largish field, of say, lavender. He finds the owner and by sweetening his way around with a bottle or two of common old gum honey, he is able to secure a standing place.

Migrating Beekeepers

To touch briefly on migrating beekeepers – this is a completely different ballgame. Again, the season starts on the 21st June and to the Aloe Davyana they go to awaken their bees from the winter rest. These low growing aloes yield a profusion of pollen and nectar from July to end of August. The hives are robbed and then moved to the citrus where they are sited until the end of October. They are then robbed again and moved to the Gauteng Highveld gum. They are robbed again at the end of January and moved to the sunflower or the kidney beans where they remain until the frost at the beginning of May. They are robbed here and then moved to resting holding sites until the aloes again at the beginning of July.

Migrating beekeepers often rest a third of their total number of swarms by leaving them on permanent apiaries for the entire year. However this is a specialist ball game for only experienced beekeepers.

The calendar on the following page is a guide as to what is flowering and where throughout the year. It is intended to assist the beekeeper (based in Gauteng) to plan ahead and to maintain a honey flow as long as possible.

Tales of an African Beekeeper

SEASONAL CALENDAR

Area	Jan	Feb	Mar	Apr	May	Jun	Jul	Aug	Sep	Oct	Nov	Dec
Eastern Highveld, east of Springs to Ermelo	Cosmos. Wild pink statice in grasslands. Blackjacks. Kidney beans in patches on farms around Delmas and in greater areas around Ermelo. Sunflower (scattered plantings). Eucalyptus camaldulensis (red river gums).											
	Acacia Karoo (Soetdoring / Sweet Thorn)		Sunflower (large plantings around Settlers)	Eucalyptus Sideroxilyn (black ironbark)							Acacia Karoo (Soetdoring / Sweet Thorn)	
Gauteng throughout	Acacia Karoo (Soetdoring / Sweet Thorn)							Eucalytus melliodora (Highveld gum)			Acacia Karoo (Soetdoring / Sweet Thorn)	
								General garden flowers				
Piet Retief + Lowveld		Eucalytus grandis (saigna)										
Lowveld: Nelspruit, Barberton, Waterval Onder through the Elands valley.								Tropical fruits, wild plums, apricots, pears, marulas, litchi, citrus, macadamia nuts				
Rustenburg						Aloe daveyana		Citrus				
Groblersdal							Aloe daveyana	Citrus				

<u>Notes</u>

36 Appendix D: Queen rearing (the Hopkins method)

Queens are the focal point of either success or failure of the swarm. This, in turn, affects honey crop, and it is an area of keeping bees where one can have control. There are many books on the subject and complicated methods are expressed involving all manner of gadgets to be used. One can read about some of these mind boggling methods, but here in South Africa there is a simple method that bypasses all this haberdashery and allows one to get on with the job.

It is a method that can be employed by a shaky, all-thumbs old beekeeper with poor eyesight and touching his early nineties.

Hopkins was an American beekeeper who enjoyed experimenting with his bees and devised a system known as "The Hopkins Method of Raising Queens". Slight modifications to his method have been made in this chapter.

Equipment required

Construct out of wood, a tray 73mm deep and to Langstroth hive size that will fit on top of a super chamber. The tray is to house a brood frame in a horizontal position so that the bottom surface of the comb is 35mm above the tops of the super frames after this tray has been placed on top of the super chamber. These dimensions are critical to prevent the bees from adhering the new queen cells to the tops of the super frames. How simple – this is the only equipment required.

Method

The best time for this operation to start is in the early spring, at the beginning of August.

1) Select a strong hive from the apiary that has given a good honey production return. This means to say that the queen prodigy is a good strain and this good stock is what we require.

2) In the brood chamber, remove an outside frame that will contain honey. Move the centre frames to the outside to create a space for a new frame to be placed in the centre of the brood rearing area.

3) Prepare a brood frame with a full sheet of foundation wax and place this frame in the centre of the brood area in the space created.

4) After the lapse of a week inspect this new frame. We require the wax foundation to have been drawn out by the bees and developed into worker cells and laid with eggs. If this is not the case then replace the frame and inspect again after a further five days, and then after a further three days until the eggs or very young larvae appear at the bottom of the cells.

   Very important! DO NOT LET THE SUN SHINE DOWN INTO THESE CELLS. The ultra violet rays can kill this very young brood.

5) Select the best side of the frame and destroy three rows of cells along the bottom bar of the frame. Reason being that we do not desire the new queen cells to be attached to the woodwork of the bottom bar of the frame.

6) Very gently place this frame into the tray in a horizontal position and place the tray on top of the super chamber and under the lid. Seal around the lid to tray, and around the tray to super chamber joints with masking tape. Reason for this is to quickly seal off draughts to this new incubation area of queen cells.

7) Now we split the hive. Pick up the hive and move it about one meter away from its original standing position.

8) Place a loose floor in the original position of the standing place of the hive. Remove the super, Hopkins tray and lid from the hive and place them intact onto the loose floor.

9) Place a new lid onto the original brood chamber and move it about three meters away and to face in another direction as before.

10) Now we have created a new swarm of worker bees and the original field force from the original swarm. After five or so hours, the bees will start to construct queen cells because of the queenless state of the new swarm. These cells will hang down vertically below the horizontal Hopkins frame.

11) The following day, after 12 hours, return the brood chamber to its original standing position, replace the queen excluder, then the super containing the Hopkins tray on the top under the lid. Once the bees have been induced to rear queen cells there is no stopping them although there is a queen present in the brood chamber well down below this Hopkins tray.

12)   The entire field worker force will have been returned to the original swarm and the bees will carry on as if nothing had happened.

Note! A GOOD QUALITY QUEEN EXCLUDER MUST BE USED – should the queen get to these cells, she will destroy them.

13)   Some cells will be attached to one another as doubles, and others individually scattered around the frame. So decide how many one is able to utilize and back to the workshop we hasten, not to miss a day now. If we are able return the same day so much the better.

14)   We have decided to utilize say eight queen cells that look the best and we are able to find eight super chambers from other hives in the apiary that we can utilize. Armed with eight loose floors and eight lids back to the apiary we hasten. By this time there will be a lot less bees around to harass the beekeeper as they will have returned to their original swarm.

15)   Remove the tray and the lid, invert the tray, and deal with one queen cell at a time. Cut out the queen cell with some brood frame comb attached behind it. Remove a super from one of the other hives, place on a loose floor and between the two centre frames, jamb the comb and queen cell combination in order that the cell hangs vertically between the frames. Close this unit with a lid and load onto the transport to be taken to another apiary where the queen cell will hatch. In the same manner, one by one we deal with each of the other remaining queen cells.

This concludes the entire operation and we have eight new swarms. As these super chambers only have nine frames one needs to transfer the frames into a brood box as soon as possible and provide ten frames to create the correct spacing for proper brood rearing. Over the duration of two or three months the shallow super frames can be exchanged for deep brood frames.

<u>Notes</u>

37 Appendix E: Taking off a 'nuc'

A nucleus box is known around beekeepers as a 'nuc', and here follows a description of how to "take off a nuc", as it is expressed.

Nuc boxes must have unattached bottoms. Some boxes have lids and bottoms that are exactly the same and can be used as a lid or a bottom. A small entrance only 25mm wide is sufficient, and when used as a lid this small opening can be plugged with sponge or left open in hot weather as a ventilator.

A nuc is the start of the development of a new swarm from a parent swarm. It is a delicate operation where one wants a small balanced swarm. That is a swarm with sealed brood, hatching brood and eggs to raise a new queen. It needs drones, so a little drone brood is not out of place. Most importantly it needs nurse or newly hatched bees. These bees secret the royal jelly required for feeding the queen cell larva, and all this in a small compact box to make the bees feel secure.

Taking off a nuc is not a one-day operation, but rather a two-day operation. The operation is best carried out when a honey flow is on the go or just prior to a honey flow. For example, at the start of the cosmos flow which will last for about 10 weeks, or the gum flow in August which lasts for 12 weeks, or ahead of any other flow.

One needs about a 30 day period to build up the swarm, which is then transferred to a brood box. One could only expect a super of honey after 90 days and for this reason the springtime take off is best for honey in February and March. However there are other ways to speed things up a bit.

A nuc is best taken off a strong colony, that is a colony with seven to eight frames of brood and a super three quarters filled with honey. Smoke the swarm and remove the lid and super together not to separate the lid from the super. We do not even want the worker bees to know that we are working on the hive. This operation does not disturb over 50% of the bees. Place this super onto a board to keep the bees contained in the super. Now gently remove the queen excluder without bumping the bees as if on a trampoline.

From the second frame start selecting suitable material – we need one open unsealed brood with young eggs. This frame will become the nurse bees for our queen rearing so therefore the more eggs and unsealed brood the better.

The second frame we need must be capped brood, also the more the better. This brood will hatch and becomes the frame to care for the developing grubs in frame number one.

The third frame can be the outside frame in the brood which will contain pollen and honey to feed the young bees, grubs and present nurse bees. At this stage this frame is easiest removed rather than at the very beginning.

The fourth frame must contain eggs and one day old larva from which the bees will draw a queen cell.

Replace the four brood frames with half foundation or clean drawn comb into the vacant space that was created. Do not disturb the remaining frames in the brood nest. It is a good idea to mark these frames for later identification. Replace the queen excluder and place the nuc box over the undisturbed half of the brood nest. We have now converted the horizontal brood nest to a vertical brood nest with a queen excluder between. We do not want the queen to be able to enter the "above" brood nest section. The nurse bees now operate in an "above and below" brood nest. As two nucs fit side by side over the width of the brood chamber, place a dummy nuc with a thin cardboard lid alongside the new nuc with its sliding bottom intact. If one is using a loose bottom, then a thin false bottom must seal off this dummy nuc. Ultimately the two top levels of the nucs must be equal. Place the super on the top of these two nucs. One now removes the sliding bottom to the new nuc to allow the worker bees to pass and carry on their nectar storing and the nurse bees to attend to the brood in the new nuc.

Now a new small balanced brood chamber has been created above the queen excluder. On the second or third day but not later, return to the scene. Smoke the hive well. Slide the sliding bottom below the new nuc and close the entrance to the nuc. Remove the super and roof and the two nucs intact, strap and load to be removed to another site at least five kilometers away. Place a drawn comb super and queen excluder onto the mother swarm. After ten days check for capped queen cells. If there are queen cells, leave undisturbed for 30 days. By this time there should be a young laying queen and some capped brood.

If there are no queen cells, there is the possibility of black pseudo queen invasion. If there are no "black pseudo queen bees" visible on close inspection one can shake the bees out in front of a weak swarm or just into the apiary. These bees will find their way to a hive of their choice. However, if any "black pseudo queen bees" are seen, the entire swarm must be destroyed.

After the 30 day period one can transfer the nuc into a brood chamber and add the missing six frames to make up the compliment of the new brood chamber. If one could add another frame or three of sealed brood from another hive, this new swarm would really have a good kick start on its way to eventual honey production.

Alternatively where there is no super over a strong brood box one draws the frame material as before above and place the new nuc over the undisturbed half of brood in the brood box. Place a half lid over the area of the brood box next to the nuc that covers the other half. After the second day, remove the new nuc and close down as described before. Add frames to the mother brood to make up the compliment to ten frames. Two or three frames from another swarm would add that little TLC to mother brood. Do not place a super over mother brood. Rather wait until the mother brood is well filled with bees before adding a super.

38 Appendix F: Frequently Asked Questions

38.1 FAQ from Farmers

In my travels I have had many encounters with farmers who would like to understand more about the implications of having bees on their farmers. Here follow a number of the most frequently asked questions I've been asked.

Q: My neighbouring farmer has hives on his property. What's that about?

A: Well, there are a number of reasons that there might be bee camps on his land, both of which are mutually beneficial.

In the first instance, it might be that a beekeeper has asked to set up a camp amongst some trees, or what we call 'a wood lot', as a source of nectar for his bees to sustain them until time for pollination of a crop on another farm. An example is that bees love eucalyptus and to have such a camp is great for the honey producer. The beekeeper could well pay the farmer for this – in cash or in kind. The farmer could get a plentiful supply of first grade honey for giving a beekeeper access to the land, receiving as much as a bottle of honey per hive per year. That's a lot of honey!

In my experience the farmers don't want money, so if they don't want that much honey they may look to you to provide some other product of value.

The farmer will however not allow the beekeeper to store too many hives there, say 150 instead of 500, so that the bees do not become a problem to his neighbour. Of course the bees may not be a problem to this farmer down the road if he is growing a similar crop, such as sunflowers, that needs pollination.

In the second instance the farmer may not have a wood lot and therefore not have a beekeeper knocking on his door.   He would often phone the local beekeepers' association to find some beekeepers, and then be contracting the beekeeper to have his bees pollinate his crops at that time of year. In this case the farmer will be paying the beekeeper a fee per hive, and this can be very beneficial to the beekeeper. Without renting the bees or having his own swarms the crop pollination is going to be much more of a hit and miss affair. If the crop is one that is going to also produce honey, such as the sunflower, then it is often the case that there is no payment in either direction because both parties benefit from the relationship.

If the crop, such as berries, is not going to provide honey because it has only pollen and not nectar, then the beekeeper is going to charge the farmer the equivalent of what he would have received if the hive had produced honey for the time of the pollination. For example if that hive was on a sunflower crop for six weeks it would yield about 20 kilograms of honey, and he wants to be compensated for that opportunity cost. Once he explains this to the farmer, the farmer can usually see that he is not being over-charged and that he is paying fair value for the service.

Tales of an African Beekeeper

Q: What are the risks of having your hives on my farm?

A: It is true that there are risks to you, and some we can minimize and others are just natural. There are primarily two types of intruder you might find because of hives – the vandal and the honey badger. The vandal doesn't know a whole lot about bees, but he does know that there is honey to be had if he gets it right. Often they will foolishly vandalize the hives with bees around, and take their chances with being attacked. But to you this means trespassers, or sometimes it is your own workers doing the deed. A risk directly linked to this is that the smarter vandals know that if they start fires they have a better chance of getting in and out of the hives without the stings.

For our part, we can try to make our hives tamper-proof with extra steel bands and reinforcement, putting up rudimentary fencing, and placing hives on stilts and not at ground level. This is something of a deterrent once word gets around, but the fact is that it pushes up our production costs. Of course, having hives wrecked instead is also an extremely costly problem for us.

Another risk that you are faced with is possible ignorance of the beekeeper when it comes to locating his hives in the wood lot. It is more accurate to speak of placing the hives next to but away from the trees. This is because of the fire risk of vandals attempting to burn the bees. It is better, and common practice with experienced beekeepers, to create firebreaks and stagger the hives at least three meters from the nearest grasses.

Q: What problems do you encounter with natural vandals such as badgers and baboons ?

A: The average male badger weighs about nine kilogams, slightly larger than the female. They live in vacated burrows in the ground and are mainly nocturnal and are most easily seen at dusk as they come out for the night life, which they enjoy when others are at a disadvantage in the dark. They are carnivorous and apart from lizards, rats and mice, farmer's chickens, they will catch anything up to a small buck. They are strong ferocious little beasties, have the sharpest set of incisor teeth along the sides and front of their mouth, and a very strong pair of front leg claws. Beware when catching one as they are able to turn 180 degrees within their skin and easily bite off a thumb as quick as a wink. They rear one youngster per year, always under the tender care of the mother for 16 months and when one sees two together it is usually mother and teenager as she teaches the sibling to hunt. Otherwise they are loners and will prowl over vast square kilometers for food, not remaining in one place for more than a day. But they will stay and take the farmer's last free range chicken before moving on. Should they come across an apiary of 50 hives, they will stay around until they have destroyed the last hive.

The badger is a natural enemy of the bees, in as much as he wants their brood, rated as their delicacy, before their honey, and also an enemy of the beekeeper as he can absolutely wreck the hive to satisfy his quest. The badger, unlike the vandal, does not come from outside of your farm. He is there naturally, and that is not something you can change. We, the beekeepers are just that jump ahead of this fellow. We know that the badger is vulnerable and loses the power in his front leg claws once he has two legs off the ground, and by placing our hives on stands 600 mm high we have beaten him. However along comes his ally, the baboon who pushes the hives over and off the stands. The badger breaks open the hives and the baboon also feasts on the honey spoils. To beat this situation, the beekeeper places the hive on a stand and straps the complete unit to a tree, stout fence pole or two stout steel stakes hammered into the ground to strap and secure the hive.

Q: What does giving you access to my farm mean to me?

A: We are all too aware of the current security risks faced by farmers (in South Africa), and that you don't want to have strangers moving about on your farm without some kind of control. It is very important that you check out the beekeeper, getting references if it helps you feel comfortable working with him. Ask him for his Association's details and of other farmers he has worked with. Maybe even get another beekeeper's reference on him.

One of the reasons why the farmer doesn't want beekeepers on his farm at night is because, when the beekeeper gets stuck in the mud, it's the farmer who is called upon to help out. The farmer doesn't want to leave his secure compound at night to help us out, for several reasons. One is that he is leaving the safe zone that he has created around the farmhouse, second is that he doesn't know exactly where you are if it is a call for help, and thirdly he doesn't know if you are alone, with labourers, or if your labourers are on their own.

The fact that many farmers don't want us working at night or 'after dark' anymore, is a great pity because that is when the bees are most docile and easy to move. We therefore have to devise means of moving the bees during the day time. This has its upside though, because whereas we weren't allowed to be on the farm during the day and had to work the midnight shift, we now have the freedom to move about in the day. However, we now have to strap the hives down, seal the sides of the hives, cover them with netting, put screens into the hives. This is also not altogether a bad thing, because it forces us to tighten up on our business – no room for wasteful practices.

Q: What about inexperienced beekeepers? They have basic training but don't know more of the details. How does that hurt the industry?

A: Bees are a dangerous livestock to have around on the farm and are feared because of the many instances of mishaps to the farmer's families and animals. Hives brought onto farms, even as far as two kilometers away, by visiting beekeepers will cast many new swarms. These swarms are attracted to farm structures and buildings and create a problem for the farmer.

Only experienced beekeepers are able to deal with complicated swarm removals. The farmers therefore hesitates to associate with inexperienced beekeepers to deal with these matters and fear that they will leave the farmer with a more serious problem should they fail to remove the swarm successfully.

Tales of an African Beekeeper

A closing remark about farmers: farmers are a wonderful society of folk. They know their neighbors over a radius of as far as 20 kilometers and they share their burdens of hardships and rejoice to share their successes. After church on Sundays they would gather in the church hall for coffee and fellowship and if called to assist a fellow farmer, they will respond without hesitation. To belong to such a community is uplifting to the most depressed, helping to wash away all grief and hardships, and it is in this caring environment that a beekeeper is accepted.

38.2 *FAQ from Gardening Enthusiasts*

In my many years with the bees I have had occasion to speak at gatherings of garden enthusiasts and home owners, and to individuals, and here I would like to list some of the most common questions I am asked. I have tried to give them a logical sequence even thought they are not all asked and not all at the same time.

Q: Why are bees important for me in my garden?

A: Well, they aren't really *important* to the garden, but they are beneficial. They have a multiple number of flowers that they visit, not doing a pollination service for mankind, but they are pollinating the flowers so that the plants can reproduce themselves, for their own survival. Their importance comes from the fact that they are reproducing the plant life in your garden and many others. They are there to collect nectar and make honey and fill the beekeeper's pockets with honey (No hun, no mun ,no fun!)

Q: But what if there are no bees in my garden?

A: If there are no bees in your garden you would be concerned if you are a serious gardener. Concerned not so much because your garden needs the bees, but that a lack of bees is a bad sign for the ecosystem. Of course that is a broader issue than just concerns the gardening enthusiast, but you might like to find out what is going on. What is your neighbour's experience? What has she seen lately? What plants does she have that you don't? Could it be that none of your plants are attractive to the bee? Or could it be that you are just not noticing those that are there, because they come at times of day that you aren't out there?

Tales of an African Beekeeper

Q: If there are no bees, and I want to encourage bees, what can I do to attract them to my garden?

A: There is a host of garden plants that you can plant that are appealing to bees. Your local nursery should be able to give you a list of such plants, and if after they flower you still have no bees, then there is a problem in your area. Bees play an important role in our country, and we would not like to hear of areas where bees have packed up and left, or died en masse.

It might be as simple as the fact that you have a green garden, a foliage garden, and just by looking at what is working at your friends' or neighbours' home you can come away with some ideas.

You might not know that, funnily enough, blue and yellow plants are known to attract bees more than red. This is because bees' visual spectrum doesn't see red – in that sense they are colour blind. However, I have found Anasodontea (pink malva) a great plant for attracting bees. It has little pink flowers and the bees absolutely love it – they are on it from early morning until very late in the day. It secretes nectar all through the temperatures of the day. I reckon that an orchard of that would produce a lot more honey than an orchard of citrus trees. It is inclined to be a bit weedy, so if you plant too much of it you might create a weed problem. It handles frost, takes drought, handles moisture.

There is also a tree list – bees gather more nectar from trees than flowers. If you look at the street trees, those on the pavements, they may be full of bees.

Q: If I am successful in attracting bees to the garden, I don't want to create a problem for myself and suddenly have the bees move in and start a hive – what do I do?

A: Well, firstly, the average garden isn't going to have enough plants to attract a swarm of bees. It would take a significant amount of plants to attract a swarm. You won't be doing harm to yourself by attracting bees to your garden.

Q: I have a fear of bees, or of lots of bees, and I hear stories about swarms and swarming. With encouraging the bees into my garden, am I increasing the risks of swarming?

A: No, not really. Swarms move when they already know where they are going. The scouts have been out there and found a suitable new home for the swarm, and they are en route. They may stop in one place along the way for a day or two, even up to four days while the queen rests, but they don't just swarm out of nowhere.

The bees you hear in the trees, for example, are just doing a job of work – they are not interested in you. While they are going about their business you could go and stand among them and they won't touch you. Of course, one has to not cause too much of a disturbance going in and out, but you would usually be left well alone.

However, what you do have to watch out for is scouts in your garden. When you see just a few bees hovering over some small crevice or dark spot in an airbrick, your shed, or toolbox, or bird box, be very wary. If these bees are not hovering around plants for nectar and pollen, then they could be scouting for a new home for the swarm.   If they like that place they will go and bring their swarm. In that event the swarm isn't going to go and hang somewhere on your house, they are going to move straight into their new home. Once they are in there is nothing you can do except call the beekeeper or live in harmony with them.

Of course, you can pre-empt their move proactively and block the hole they are going to use, or paint it with some Jeyes fluid (carbolic cleaning fluid). They really don't like the smell of dishwashing liquid either, so you could spray that in and around the hole too. So, the bottom line is that you want to be observant but not obsessive about bee activity in your garden surrounds, and you can do things to head them off.

Q: Are there different times of day that bees are most active?

A: Yes, but more because of the plants than the bees. Different plants secrete nectar at different times of the day. Some plants secrete nectar in the coolest part of the day, and some in the heat of the day.

Take citrus trees for example. They secrete nectar all day, all of the time. However, because of the coolness of the morning the nectar doesn't evaporate. But in the heat of the day, and in citrus areas it can get very hot, and the nectar evaporates leaving a sort of a powder, a crystal powder, which the bee cannot take – so she doesn't even go to those flowers. She's a clever girl our honeybee, and she isn't going to waste time flying around when there's nothing to forage at that time of day.

Similarly when pollen is available, the bees will gather pollen, but not nectar and pollen on the same foraging trip. On some days with inclement weather, the pollen can be moist and poisonous to the bee, so they won't gather it.

Q: What about pesticides that I might use which may be harmful to the bees? Now that I have a bee-friendly garden, how do I keep from killing our honey-making visitors?

A: Most pesticides nowadays are, under legislation, supposed to be bee-friendly. As a result, most of what you will buy commercially complies with the legislation, but in a few cases there are some commercial farmers who indiscriminately use pesticides which are good for their crops but bad for the bees.

So as the home garden enthusiast your insecticide is already bee friendly, but you could check with your nursery before you buy it. Of course, the irony of it all is that beekeepers will also use the non-registered poisons specifically to poison bees when absolutely necessary, and they will use these because they are most effective.

39 ABOUT THE AUTHOR

Peter Clark has been a beekeeper for some sixty years, starting off as a hobbyist, and turning it into a retirement income later in life. Peter is a man of the land and would have become a farmer if life had dealt a different hand. Instead he has been 'farming' bees successfully all these years. His business takes him all over the region, visiting farms far and wide; enjoying the various characters that beekeeping has introduced him to.

Over 70 years of age Peter still works his own hives, and has been successfully running his bee courses for many years under the auspices of the Eastern Transvaal Beekeeping Society.

He lives in Springs, historically a gold mining area east of Johannesburg, South Africa.

Peter L Clark

40 ACKNOWLEDGMENTS

There are many instructive books on beekeeping covering the "what to do" and "how to do it" but the craft can really only be learnt from fellow beekeepers. Therefore one needs to mix around with beekeepers, and I have been particularly blessed to have known and learnt from a great number of beekeepers. I wish to acknowledge the following men, who have taught me over the years.

My start was self-motivated. At the age of 16 years I decided to make a beehive. We lived on Daggafontein mine, Springs, and my first mentor was:

Bill Joiner, who gave me my first swarm in a cardboard box. I made my first hive from scrap timber and tomato box wood for the frames. This swarm developed into a very strong swarm that I could not handle and to my relief Willie Seidel, a beekeeper from Springs, removed it from our premises. Bill introduced me to another 16 year-old also interested in bees and between us we became the official beekeepers of the mine property, going about on our bicycles.

Peter Lelliette. After putting in so much effort to make this hive, another beekeeper from the mine took pity on me and gave me two standard Langstroth hives, one riddled with wax moth and the other chock-a-block full of honey. Well I cut the honey into chunks and hawked it around the mine, delighted with my efforts, as this was the very first honey I ever sold.

Twenty years slipped by and at the age of 36 years, and in 1973 I joined Eastern Highveld Beekeepers' Association and from 1976 onwards I progressed in leaps and bounds. I served on the committee for 36 years, either as Treasurer, Secretary, committee member, or Chairman, until present times of 2012, and perhaps my dedication to the association touched the hearts of many members who were willing to help me along the road to success. These folk set me on the right track, advised me, mentored me, invited me to work along with them in order for me to attain my goals, and just helped me all the way.

Hugh (Judge) Hardy. Hugh was a hardened old war horse, having been a lorry driver in the second world war with the Transvaal "Jocks" in the East African campaign. After the war he picked up beekeeping where he had left off before the war. Most fortunately for me, he taught me in depth beekeeping and for 10 years we worked together in all aspects of beekeeping (most positively my second angel).

Brett Falconer. At age 17 years, Brett formed a threesome with Hugh and myself. He became a mechanical engineer but the bee bug had bitten him as well and beekeeping was to become his life's career. At present times, year 2012, at the age of 52 years, he lives in Benoni and operates 7,000 hives under the name of Highveld Honey Farm. He has risen to become one of the leading beekeepers in South Africa. He is married, to a dear wife who shares all his hard and fast days and is the proud father of two fine sons. I am most fortunate to have such a friend for 36 years at my very doorstep, in whom I constantly confide and seek advice on a wide spectrum of beekeeping matters.

Andrew (Andy) Warroll. We worked together for eight years on sunflowers, aloes and kidney beans over a radius of 200 kilometers. Andy always maintained that he was the brains and I was the brawn and we worked

300 hives between us. We reaped about 16 tons of honey over the eight years. Andy was employed full-time with the weather bureau and upon his retirement I took over his hives and he went farming at York in Natal.

Larry Viljoen. He was a stickler for perfection, always improving and experimenting. He operated about 150 hives. We worked together for about eight years over the same 200 kilometers radius as prior with Andy. He preferred the indigenous bushveld honey and the aloe seasons to breed queens and increase his swarms to great strengths. He taught me the importance of perfection and always corrected me for poor workmanship in handling the bees. He was a gentle operator and like all of us, loved his bees. We became great friends and would go the extra mile for each other. On our last outing, we worked on bees on the Friday afternoon and sadly and suddenly Larry passed away in church on the Sunday. His passing left a great void in my life.

Frank Parish. Frank like Hugh was a pre-war beekeeper. He kept Eastern Highveld Beekeepers' Association's candle burning during the thin years of the war 1939-1945. He lived on a smallholding near Nigel and in my early learning years taught me a great deal about the habits of bees and how to recognize angry and short-tempered bees, even before attempting to open the hives. On Saturday afternoons there were many field days at Frank's place and barbeques in the early evenings. I was always delighted to be invited out to "Frank's place" with Hugh and Brett to "look at the bees". Whenever Frank spoke of "looking at the bees", we knew we were in for an afternoon's work to crop the honey.

Willie Seidel. After 20 years I eventually met up with Willie again, but by this time I was operating 600 hives. He remembered well the occasion when he removed that hive at Daggafontein and he couldn't resist reminding me that the tomato box wood frames were so poorly made that they simply collapsed when he tried to remove them. He loved his bees and taught me how to be very gentle, so as not to kill or injure a single bee when opening hives, and under his guidance I gained heaps of confidence. He loved the outdoors and would set up camp somewhere under trees or alongside a dam and stay with his bees for the duration of the honey flow. Then out in the open he would set up his petrol driven extractor and with the air abuzz with thousands of bees, he would proceed to spin out his honey. His organization was called Eidelweis Apiaries. He passed away at the age of 95 years.

George de Braak. George was an ex-building contractor and fully aware of the more downs than ups that I was experiencing in the building industry at that time, and he continually urged me to change to bee farming. He lived on a smallholding in Boksburg and operated 400 hives. He bottled and sold on average of 12,000 bottles per annum (in 2012 years terms worth about R360,000). He would load up 2,000 bottles and go on "tour" with his honey, sometimes south to Natal, sometimes north to Tzaneen, or east to Nelspruit. Sometimes he would be away for a week, sometimes two, and after selling all the honey, he would return with the money. He and his wife worked as a team. George did all the field and workshop operations and would hand over the extracted honey to his wife, Ria. She never allowed George into the bottling room wearing his dirty boots. Ria did the bottling and ran a shop on the smallholding.

There were many others but these are the folk who taught me, encouraged me, and set me up in my bee farming career that I so enjoy in these years of my mid-seventies.